YOU'LL NEVER BELIEVE
WHAT HAPPENED TO LACEY

YOU'LL NEVER BELIEVE WHAT HAPPENED TO LACEY

Crazy Stories about Racism

Amber Ruffin and Lacey Lamar

GRAND CENTRAL
PUBLISHING

New York Boston

Copyright © 2021 by Amber Ruffin and Lacey Lamar

Cover design by Alicia Tatone
Cover photo of Amber Ruffin by Lloyd Bishop; cover photo of Lacey Lamar by Emily Strauss Photography
Cover copyright © 2021 by Hachette Book Group, Inc.

Grand Central Publishing
Hachette Book Group
1290 Avenue of the Americas, New York, NY 10104
grandcentralpublishing.com
twitter.com/grandcentralpub

First edition: January 2021

Grand Central Publishing is a division of Hachette Book Group, Inc. The Grand Central Publishing name and logo is a trademark of Hachette Book Group, Inc.

The publisher is not responsible for websites (or their content) that are not owned by the publisher.

The Hachette Speakers Bureau provides a wide range of authors for speaking events. To find out more, go to www.hachettespeakersbureau.com or call (866) 376-6591.

Library of Congress Control Number: 2020946461

ISBNs: 978-1-5387-1936-7 (hardcover), 978-1-5387-1934-3 (ebook)

Printed in the United States of America

LSC-C

Printing 1, 2020

This book is dedicated to Black mothers and fathers like James and Theresa Ruffin, who teach us how to deal with racism; to Black brothers and sisters like Chrystal, Angela, and Jimmy, who provide support; and to Black children like Imani, who hopefully have it easier than we did.

And, most of all, this book is dedicated to El DeBarge. You are truly the Rhythm of the Night.

Contents

YOU'LL NEVER BELIEVE
WHAT HAPPENED TO LACEY

L acey used to have these Black history checks. Each check had a different Black hero on it. MLK, Rosa Parks, Frederick Douglass. So Lacey was at a store chatting with the cashier and they're having fun. After she's all rung up, Lacey handed the young white cashier a check with a picture of Harriet Tubman on it and the cashier said, "Wow! You have checks with your picture on 'em?" I am sorry this book peaked so early. That is the funniest story I will ever hear. Harriet Tubman, y'all. Look at their two faces! This story happened years ago and I still think about it and laugh out loud.

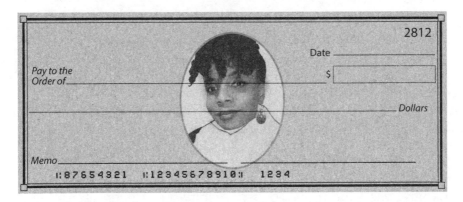

HI!

My sister Lacey is a lightning rod for hilarious racist stories. She's the perfect mix of polite, beautiful, tiny, and Black that makes people think: *I can say whatever I want to this woman.* And I guess you can. Hey, knock yourself out—but that doesn't mean you won't end up in a book.

I am not exaggerating when I say "You won't believe what happened to Lacey." And I'm hard to impress. My name is Amber Ruffin. I grew up with my big sister Lacey, our mom, dad, two other sisters, and one brother in Omaha, Nebraska. I know exactly the type of shenanigans folks will pull on a person of color. My lord, have I heard some things. But my feeble stories never come close to the hilarity that befalls Lacey on a near daily basis.

I moved away from Omaha many years ago and now I work in New York City, where I write comedy. Everyone I work with is stark raving normal. We don't have any crazy bigots (dumb enough to run up) and I'm no one's first Black friend. Now, I'm not saying no one ever says anything crazy to me—I'm still a Black woman in America—it's just that we all know there are consequences for talking to me as if you've lost your mind. So I've forgotten, more or less, the constant flow of racism one must endure to live in the Midwest and be the only Black person at work. It is an unchecked tsunami of dumb questions and comments. You're expected to walk people through every aspect of Blackness. You become the ambassador of Black-ovia. People think it's your job to answer every dumb "Why can't I (insert the most nonsense shit you've ever heard)? Is it because I'm white?" I call this process "dragging white people into the light," and it's something I don't do anymore.

This is Lacey. My little sister, Amber, is spoiled and has forgotten the 1970s-esque social blindspot she's left me in.

Don't get me wrong, I'm glad that she's gotten to move away from Omaha to New York, where someone would get fired for out-and-out racism. I love that that really happens. Never seen it, but I love it. Like Santa Claus. I've seen movies about it, heard people talk about it. I understand it's normal for a lot of people, but it would be like having a zebra in your living room for me. I would not believe my eyes.

Twice a week, I get a text from my sister that says, "Can you talk?" It's my favorite because I know I'm about to be transported to a place that exists in real life and fantasy: the place where coworkers will put their whole hand in your hair, talking 'bout "It's fluffy like a dog." I realize this sounds terrible, but it's like watching *Dateline*. You can't believe it was the GIRLFRIEND who killed the HUSBAND! It's the edge of reality. Technically, it happens, but it is barely plausible. Excited, I steal away to the elevator banks at work and listen to Lacey tell me a new horror story. It's fantastic. As I stand there, mouth agape, listening to some new fresh hell, I am always struck by the fact that these stories will only exist in this phone call. Some will go on to become stories once the topic turns to "racist people at work" one night when Lacey is hanging out with her friends, but she'll forget most of them because of the sheer volume. The. Sheer. Volume.

Now, I understand all of this sounds harsh, but you have to know that this is not a book full of sad stories. The previous paragraph was the saddest it will get for a while. Black people hear stories like these so frequently that it takes a lot for it to start to hurt our feelings. We have all been through it. But, dare I say, you ain't been through it like Lacey. Black readers will read these stories and feel that really good, yet terrible feeling of going through something bad and realizing you're not alone, and not only that, but that someone else has it worse! And, hopefully, the white reader is gonna read this, feel sad, think a little about it, feel like an ally, come to a greater understanding of the DEPTH of this type of shit, and maybe walk away with a different point of view of what it's like to be a Black American in the twenty-first century.

Hence this book.

Why? Why Would a Person Do This?

There are a few reasons why I think this book is important. I think it's important for people to speak on what has happened in their lives. When something shitty happens to you and you never say anything about it, it festers. And trying to act like it's not happening is bad for you.

I know, Lacey! This is Amber and, so you know, we are going to tell you who's who through different fonts. When you see Helvetica, it's Amber.

And when you see Bembo, it's Lacey!

You guys, Lacey has the burden of carrying around all this garbage alone. I want to unburden her. I want to wrap my hair in kente cloth, stand on a rock, and shout, "Let us unburden our sister Lacey by gathering to hear her stories, lest they drag her down to the pits of depression." But that'd be insane. Slightly less insane? Gathering these stories into a book and selling it to strangers in malls and airports throughout the country.

Also, any person who has to live like this needs to hear that there is a second person slogging through this mess. And then they'll realize that there's a lot of people living like this and feel better, then worse for a second, and then better again.

We want to use this book to make sure people understand that when something racist happens to you, you can say it. You can feel however it makes you feel and you can talk to people about it. You have the right. It can hit you however it hits you at that exact moment. You can express your feelings about it or not, or just tell the story and leave your feelings out, or just say your feelings and leave the story out—it's your world. There's a billion studies about why you should speak positively, mediate, how to handle loss, and stuff like that, but when it comes to how to live in a country made to abuse you, who the fuck knows. So do what you feel.

And not to go "full hippie" on you, but leaving these things unsaid gives them power. Try to unroll your eyes to read the rest of this: if you do not take the time out and call bad things that have happened to you "bad," they float around your brain category-less and with influence from the type of people who want to penalize you for calling racist things racist, and those events can fall into the "okay" category.

Shut up, Lacey. And finally, has anyone taken a look at a lifetime of racism? I mean, this isn't *every* racist story that has happened to her, and she's nowhere near the end of her life-time, but it's a good chunk of 'em. Some of these stories are old, but a lot of them are post-Obama stories. A lot of folks think things like this don't happen anymore. But in this climate where people are becoming more brave with their racism, I think things may get worse before they get better. Just kidding, I don't think things are gonna get better. Just kidding about just kidding. I'm Team Hopeful! My point is: Has anyone ever decided to take a look at one person's buttload of racist stories? What happens when you do? I don't know, but here you go.

About the Authors

Amber Ruffin was born in Omaha, Nebraska, in 19-whatever-year-is-plausible-for-you-but-still-implies-that-she-is-young. She moved to Chicago to pursue a career in improv and—laugh all you want—it worked! She was hired by a theater called Boom Chicago in Amsterdam, where she did improv shows for what felt like a billion years. She also did shows in Chicago at the Second City Mainstage. And that's it. That is a complete list of full-time improv jobs you can have in this world.

In 2014, Amber became the first Black woman to write for a late-night network talk show in the United States. As of her writing this, she's a writer/performer on *Late Night with Seth Meyers* and the host of *The Amber Ruffin Show* on the new

NBC streaming service, Peacock. But by the time you read this she'll be . . . king?

Lacey Lamar is Amber Ruffin's big sister. She was born in Omaha, Nebraska, and if you want to know what year, take the year you imagined me being born and subtract four years. Lacey is the middle child in our family, yet somehow the only normal one. After all the "less than fun" jobs she has had over the years, she feels she's finally found a great job as a program director at a good company. Living in Nebraska, Lacey loves the challenge of creating safe spaces for the celebration of Nerd/African American culture. See how we used the word *challenge*? Polite, huh?

Intro

P icture it: Omaha, Nebraska. 1980–2020. This is the setting all these stories take place in. It's not completely back- ward, but Omaha is still pretty segregated, so there are places you can go and get stared at. You know what I mean? Where no one talks to you and when they do, it's to ask you if you work here. It's not the most racist place but it's not the least racist place.

Okay, so just like everything, Omaha has a wide range of white people. From regular to "Look how cool I am with Black[1]

---

1   You'll notice throughout this book that I capitalize *Black* and I leave *white* lowercased. It is because, when I was in history class in seventh grade, I saw a lecture where some Black activist, I forget who, said to always capitalize Black when talking about African Americans who were descendants of slaves. The thinking was, the term *African American* is a reminder that Africa is a whole continent and we will never be able to pinpoint exactly where our ancestors were from on it. It's like saying "South American." There's a lot of frigging countries and cultures in South America; if you can't say which, you might as well say "earthling." They also said *African American* is kind of like *Polish American* in that it makes it seem like you chose to come here. Black Americans may be from the same place but how we got here is very different and we aren't ashamed of it. So we had to start embracing the whole Black American experience. We have a rich culture to draw from and feel loved by. At some point, each

people" to "Eww! A Black person!" It's never a Black person's job to make sure these people understand why what they're saying is wrong. It's our job to survive another day as a Black person in America. Sounds dramatic, but, as you will find out, it can be a tough thing to do! Lest I scare you, here's the range of these stories: No one gets hurt. No one dies. Not in this book. This book is not about those things. This book is about the stories you're expected to swallow or forget. So Bon appétit!

As I've said before, Lacey is a magnet for this behavior because she's small and nice and cute. Another factor is where these stories take place. The majority of these stories happen in Lacey's workplaces. When you're at work and someone says something crazy, you gotta walk the tightrope. You don't want to hurt their feelings so badly that they get you fired (getting a Black lady fired from your workplace is so easy you can do it accidentally!), but you also don't want to create an environment where you're a sounding board for people's gross racist thoughts. You're already the person they come to to discuss rap. That is enough.

I don't know what effect stories like these have on the people they happen to, on the people who hear them, or on the people who need to hear them. When you hear these stories

---

of our family trees turns into a pile of receipts. So, we would claim "Black" as "descendants of slaves." Does that make sense? Just kidding—I don't care if it does. Anyway, when I saw this on TV, honestly, I didn't feel very strongly about it. I understood where the activist was coming from, though. So I decided to try it out and take their advice and used it in a history paper. The teacher told me I couldn't capitalize Black and not white. He insisted that I capitalize neither. I proceeded to capitalize Black on every paper I turned in and got five points off every time. If you want to share your opinions with me on this, please write down all your thoughts on a paper airplane and throw it out your window!

and think, *None of these stories are okay*, you are right. And when you hear these stories and think, *Dang, that's hilarious*, you are right. They're both.

There are going to be a lot of times while you're reading this book when you think, *There is no motivation for this action. It seems like this story is missing a part because people just aren't this nonsensically cruel.* But where you see no motivation, you understand racism a little more. It's this weird, unprovoked lashing-out, and it never makes any sense. It's why it's so easy for people to believe the police when they beat someone up— because no one would be that cruel just because the person was Black. But they are! So, as you read this book, when you see there's no motivation, know that there is: racism.

Here's a pretty racist map of Omaha. Get familiar with it because it will be a part of a lot of these stories!

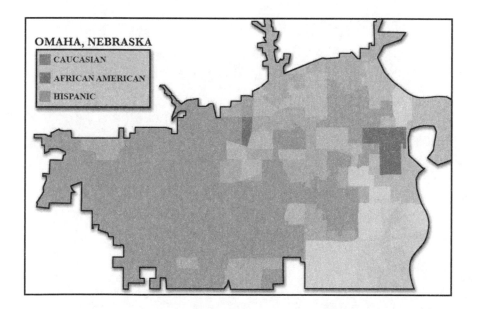

OMAHA, NEBRASKA

CAUCASIAN

AFRICAN AMERICAN

HISPANIC

Before you come to the conclusion that Omaha is some small backwoods town, here's a list of cities we are bigger than:

New Orleans, Louisiana
Oakland, California
Cleveland, Ohio
Pittsburgh, Pennsylvania
Salt Lake City, Utah
Orlando, Florida
Minneapolis, Minnesota

Omaha is the forty-fourth biggest city in America. There is no excuse for this behavior.

I Got a Million of 'Em

These are the stories we all have. If you know a Black person, odds are this has happened to them. If you are a Black person, remember that? Crazy, huh? It's a good place for this collection of stories to start. If you read this first chapter and think, *There's no way this happened! I refuse to believe it!*, then you may not be able to make it through this book.

Let's begin this book with one of the most fun and most frequent racist stories: being told you look like someone you in no way look like but is also Black. Sometimes you say, "I don't look like that person at all. You cannot see." But sometimes you say, "Fine. I do look like Michelle Obama." You can't be fighting everyone all the time. They'll have to wait for a more patient Black person to tell them they've lost their mind.

One summer in the mid '90s, I went on a vacation to Rocky Mountain National Park in Colorado. It was a fun trip through the mountains even though there wasn't another Black person in sight. I walk into a lovely store that sells trinkets and tourist

1

stuff. It's pretty darn cute. And what's even better, the lady behind the counter sees me and is happy! This does not happen a lot, period. Much less in the middle of the mountains. So this lady runs up to me, a Black lady, smiling from ear to ear. She is like, "Yay! Whoopeeee!" And I, being a natural improviser, yell right back, "Yay! Whoopity doo!" No one's ever been so happy to see me that they exclaim like that before. But this lady has me believing that those people are wrong and this is the only way I should ever be greeted. The lady runs up to me and says, "Oh my god. I can't believe you're in my store!" I'm thinking, *Who in the world does she think I am?* The lady insists that I take whatever I want—on the house! I politely thank her while I suss out the situation. Maybe she is so glad to see a Black person she wants to give me free stuff? It's possible. You never know what a white person is gonna do.

She says, "I'm your biggest fan. I've loved you since *Jumpin' Jack Flash*!" That's when I realize this woman thinks I'm Whoopi Goldberg. She was yelling "Whoopi" as in "Goldberg," not "Whoopeee" as in "Yippidee doo." Now, this woman doesn't just think I look like her, which happens to both of us a lot, but she thinks I *am* her. Now I'm having quite a conundrum. It is not right to take T-shirts that are meant for Whoopi Goldberg. But, on the other hand, free T-shirts. Who was I to reject this compliment? I love Whoopi Goldberg! I look into the lady's eyes and realize that Whoopi Goldberg being in her store has made her year. It would be wrong not to take five T-shirts and leave. So I do.

Here are some pictures of people I have been told I look like next to pictures of me trying my best to look like them.

SOME "NO SERVICE" STORIES

Lacey loves Omaha Fashion Week. She goes every year. Omaha Fashion Week is a big deal fashion show and expo where Omaha showcases a lot of its talented designers. It's really fun and Lacey loves supporting local businesses.

I think it's inspiring to see what my neighbors have come up with! They're right here, in Omaha!

Y'all, this nerd loves Omaha and all our events and fund-raisers and gatherings. She's a nerd for Omaha events.

So do you!

Oh my god, I do! We are both nerds.

One year, Lacey went with friends and the whole show was fun, but she became fixated on one specific designer. Her dresses were amazing. Lacey started to think, *Amber needs one of these for the Emmys!* (I love to go every year to lose.) At the end of the show you can meet the designers and ask how to purchase different pieces. There's a long line to wait in to meet this designer. Lacey doesn't care; she's mesmerized by glamour! She waits the fifteen minutes in line to talk to her and when she gets to the front she meets her associate. Lacey asks if she can meet the designer, who is standing a few feet away. The associate says to Lacey, "Her pieces are really expensive." In no way was that an answer to her question. Now, a few things could be happening here.

Possibility 1: This could be your traditional white person who thinks Black people spend too much on stuff we can't afford. It feels good for them to tell Black people they can't afford things because treating grown Black men and women like children makes them feel superior.

Or:

Possibility 2: This could be that thing where white people don't want to be associated with you because it would make people think less of them. Maybe they want to be known as a very bougie brand and they think that Black people wearing their clothes will do the opposite.

Or:

Possibility 3: We found a mean old bitch who was smack dab in the middle of being a mean old bitch.

Or:

Possibility 4: They're just looking out for you. Just kidding. I put this here just so you know that this category is exactly Possibility Number One!

Doesn't matter what's going on here. She's not the designer. Lacey ignores her. She even has pity for the designer for having an asshole of an assistant. Surely this designer whose clothes spoke to Lacey's *soul* would be different. Lacey walks right up to the designer and says, "Hello! Are you the designer?" Without missing a beat, this woman says, "These are exclusive, one-of-a-kind runway pieces and they're very expensive." Well, what do you fucking know? All this while Lacey thought she was in Omaha. Turns out, she had walked into an Armani fashion show! So sorry, Donatella Versace. She thought she was supporting her community! Whoops! Excuse me, Gucci! I thought this was the kind of fashion show that was open to the public where people stand in a line and get to talk to the designer! Sorry for wanting to tell you you're great and purchase your dresses. That's Omaha.

Lacey loudly replies, "Wow, you're really rude. Is that how you talk to Black people? Well, thanks, because your attitude just saved me"—looks at the price tag—"575 dollars! 575 dollars? This only costs 575 dollars? Wow. I thought this was supposed to be a runway piece. Thank goodness I didn't buy this. I could have really embarrassed myself."

There is this very insane Black thing where people out loud will assume you have no money by just looking at you. Especially if you ask how much something costs. Sometimes when you ask, "How much is this?" people hear, "Do I have any business buying it?" It makes you wanna scream. No one is asking you to look at them and guess if they can afford it; people wanna know the frigging price! Do white people not ask what things cost? Ha ha ha—but also, for real, do they?

Mom and Angie recently went to the grocery store together. And at this point, early in the book, I just want to say I am struck by how many of these stories happened *after* we sold this book. I mean, there were more than enough stories before we sold the book. But dang, I'm now realizing that like ten percent of these stories are brand-spankin'-new! Okay, all I'm saying is this is a lot. All right, so Mommy and Angie. They thought they might make lobster for the two of them. No one else in the family really likes it. In the fish department, they asked the guy how much lobster tails are and the Great Lobster Keeper replied, "They're really expensive." And it's like, I didn't ask you if *you* can afford a lobster tail. I asked how much they are! This shit is maddening. Mom mean-mugged this man and growled, "I'll take four." Instantly he knew what he had done.

They watched as he silently packed up the four tails. The two of them ate lobster, like, six different ways. Now, are we rich? No. Can we afford to buy two frigging lobster tails at a dang supermarket one time? Yeah. But now that you've acted like a fool, we gotta eat four.

Lacey went to a car dealership to buy a car. She was prepared to be harassed like car dealers do. To constantly be followed around. She walked in and there were no customers, so everyone was really into helping her. Not exactly what she wanted.

Actually, I kind of love going to car dealerships because it is one of the few places where, even though you're Black, people fall all over themselves to help you.

It's probably what being white is like.

It's fun, but I wouldn't want that all the time.

Too much.

Can you imagine getting that service everywhere you went? Why, constantly being treated like you're really important would turn you into a . . . a . . .

A WHITE WOMAN?

Did we just figure out why Karens Karen?

Yes, we did.

Anyway, Lacey immediately found the exact car she wanted, so there was nothing to do but search their inventory to compare each model to see which color and options were available. She goes into the office with one of the salesmen and slowly the place starts to get customers. There's one customer for each salesman. Lucky! As Lacey sits in the office with her salesman, he's putting in options on his computer to see which car has what she wants. The guy is moving kind of slow and, while Lacey doesn't mind, this guy's boss is pacing outside his office. He is so annoyed and Lacey sees why. There is an additional customer who is not being helped. Now, instead of this man helping the additional customer himself, he wants this guy to do it, for some reason. His pacing is making Lacey's salesman nervous. He says, "Let me ask my boss how to look this up." And goes to talk to the pacing guy. The pacing guy points to the new customers and Lacey's salesman goes to help them. Now there are three new customers waiting to be helped. The boss comes in to the office and says to Lacey, "I don't think we have what you're looking for." Y'all. A car salesman had a sure thing and chose not to make a sale. He would rather roll the dice with the people who just walked in than sell a car to this woman with her fucking checkbook out. This is what Lacey gets for walking in there worried that she would get too much help! Too much help! I honestly can't imagine.

Omaha has a giant furniture store. This place is huge. It's, like, a couple of blocks big. It's so big and has so many employees that you never know what kind of service you're gonna get. The whole shtick of the place was that it was owned by a supercute little old lady. She would appear in the commercials and it was adorable. Once, a million years ago, my parents bought a bedroom set from the showroom. They noticed that the bedroom set on the showroom floor was broken. They were assured that the one that would be delivered to their house would be perfect. But they delivered the broken one, and it fell apart. So my parents drove to this store to talk to someone about it. When they get there, absolutely no one will talk to them. So they demand to see the boss. And, for some reason, they let them! Mom and Dad walk into the office of the woman who owns this place. The real live sweet old lady from all of the commercials! She's at her desk doing some work. My parents walk in and say, "Hello. We bought a bedroom set and when it was delivered, it completely fell to pieces." The sweet old lady looks up from her work at my two Black parents and, without saying a word, waves them away. They leave and nothing gets fixed.

Anyhoo, Lacey is at this furniture store. It's literally decades later; I'm sure it's gotten better. She sees a coffee table she is in love with. She looks for a price tag and there is none. She finds an employee and asks how much the coffee table is. Wouldn't you know it, this bitch says, "Expensive," and walks away. I mean, we are all on Lacey's side here, but that is a straight-up hilarious thing to say.

Amber!

It is, though.

Yeah. I guess you're right.

Agree to both think it's funny and hate it?

Agreed.

Lacey is hot. She looks for a manager, finds one, and tells him what happened. The manager, completely missing the point, says, "I'll look it up for you." Fine. She's mad, but also, how much is this coffee table? Why is this so hard? This manager finds the price and looks up from the screen and says, "Wow. It IS expensive!" Now, Lacey is fucking livid. She yells, "Ring it up." Silently, the manager does. You guys. Y'all. You guys. The table was two hundred dollars. That is not what expensive is. Not for a coffee table. Also, again, don't you want to sell these? Tell me I'm getting a great deal, you frigging idiot! It has to be said that we have all gone to this furniture store before and since and were treated perfectly. It was an anomaly that Lacey found two dum-dums in a row.

Maybe my favorite story about this is: Once, Lacey's best friend, Laura, asked how much a Rolex was. The lady who worked at the fancy watch store said, "I'm sorry, it's really expensive." Laura replied, "Bitch, I'll take two." She got two.

I would bet this next story is one every Black woman in America has: Once, Lacey was walking through a department store in a mall. She hears music and sees lights and notices a big crowd over by the makeup counter. They're doing makeovers and there's a fashion show! Fun! Lacey watches one makeup artist doing a great job. She gives her customer this crazy eye makeup. Lacey's in love. She's determined to get that look. She doesn't care how long she has to wait in line. She walks up to the makeup artist and says, "I love this lady's eye makeup. How long would it take to do mine? "The lady looks at Lacey with full confidence and says, "It would take a while, but I would love to do that for you!" Cool! Lacey waits in line while the artist does other people's makeup. This lady is doing an excellent job. Lacey is the only Black person in line, but that can't be a problem. The lady was so nice and superconfident!

When it's finally Lacey's turn, she sits in the chair and the makeup artist says, "Close your eyes." Lacey assumes she's starting on her eyes. But she feels her applying foundation. No matter the makeup person's confidence, it's always a toss-up with foundation. More often than not, lines of makeup simply don't have your color, or the makeup artist doesn't know how to find it, or both. Not what Lacey asked for and also not necessary. Lacey rarely leaves the house without a full face. But whatever. It'll be fine. Lacey opens her eyes after her foundation is applied. And the first thing she sees is a white man standing across the way. He is looking at her the same way you would look at someone who was being hacked into a million pieces. This man is horrified. It is the same look that was on your face when you were watching the movie *Alien* and saw the alien burst outta that guy's chest. It's just makeup, but this man looks terribly concerned. Lacey doesn't know him, but his face says it all. Something is very wrong. Before she closes her eyes for the makeup lady to apply the eye shadow, the man looks right at Lacey and shakes his head no. Lacey knew to be scared. It's too late now. In for a penny, in for a pound. As she is applying the eye shadow, the artist is saying things like

"It won't look EXACTLY the same as the other lady because of the difference in your skin tones." Lacey responds, "Yep." She can feel her applying a thick layer of eye shadow from her eyelashes all the way up to her eyebrow. Whatever she's doing, Lacey can feel it's wrong. She's scared. When it's over, the lady hands Lacey the mirror. Lacey has never been so mortified in her life. The white guy is still there. They lock eyes. He is very sad in his heart, but he musters a *Hang in there, champ* kind of smile. Lacey is in whiteface. Her foundation is five shades too light. Just because you used the darkest foundation you have doesn't mean it is dark enough. By the way, this is an ever-present struggle. To this day, some makeup lines you just can't use.

She used a color called White Person in a Tanning Booth.

Not only was Lacey now a white woman, but her poor eye shadow. The lady did not come close to making Lacey's eyes look like the previous customer's. Lacey had a thick square of black eye shadow on each eye. No lipstick, no blush—just a ghost with black eyes. Lacey may not be the best at putting on makeup, but this she could have done herself. When Lacey told the artist the foundation wasn't dark enough, she explained it was the darkest she had.

As she walked away, Lacey was stopped by a makeup artist at a different booth who grabbed her and said, "We need to fix this." They laughed as she cleaned Lacey's face up. The makeup artist said, "I've never seen anything like this before." Lacey: "I'm a magnet for this stuff."

Luckily, Lacey re-created the look just for us.

"BEEEWARE WHO YOU LET DO YOUR MAKEUP! YOU COULD END UP HAUNTING THE MALL LIKE IIII DOOOOOO!"

YOUR NAME MAY BE ON THE LIST, BUT BECAUSE OF YOUR FACE, I'LL NEVER CHECK!

Lacey loves going to Omaha events. It's a fun chance to get dressed up, have a good time, and donate to a good cause. Lacey has a good friend who is often able to put her on the list. But almost every single time she goes, it's the same. She walks up to the ticket table, tells them her name, they pretend to look, and they tell her there is no ticket waiting for her and her name is not on the list. But it is. It always is. She wouldn't be coming up to them if it weren't.

Ice-T was in Omaha headlining a fund-raiser for a children's home. They thought Lacey was not on the list because tickets were expensive. She was on the list.

Lacey went to a health-care seminar—not a fancy fund-raiser, a health-care seminar—and when she gave her name to the woman, without looking down she said, "Are you in the right place? This is a health-care seminar!" She was on the list.

At a fund-raiser for the Girl Scouts, the ticket person gave her such a hard time that she almost didn't get in! They went back and forth for a while. Lacey had to call her friend over to help her. She was on the list. She got in and right inside the door there were a few racks to hang your coats. As she hung her coat, a line formed behind her. People thought she was the coat-check girl! If she were smart, she would have stayed, taken coats, and made a few dollars. Instead, she told them she was not the coat-check girl.

WHITE GUYS TRYING THEIR BEST

Dating apps are fun! As long as it's your sister doing the dating and getting the insane messages from strangers and sending you screenshots of them. When you're on a dating app, anyone can send you messages. Even white guys who shouldn't be. Here's a little section of the book about that very phenomenon!

Every Black person has been hit on by someone who makes it all about race. Speaking of "all about race"—this book! Okay, so imagine your name is Thor. Your parents were hippies; that's why they chose that name. That's not the point. Imagine how many times someone has learned your name and immediately made jokes about you being a god or lightning or thunder or hammers. By the time you're ten, you've heard it all. That's kind of what it's like being Black. That and constant oppression. A white person thinks of a Black joke and immediately tells you. They think the situation you're in together is special. It is not. They think they can come up with a Black joke you haven't heard some iteration of before. They cannot. They think it shows you they're comfortable with your Blackness. Nope. They think it's fun for anyone involved. Big, juicy no. Even when I was eight, the last time I heard a new Black joke for the first time, it wasn't fun. It has never been. It just reminds me that my being Black is on your mind when you see me. This isn't about how a Black joke from a Black person can be affirming and fun and familiar and insightful. This is about how a Black joke from a white person is always exactly none of those things.

Hello there, how are you? I hope you are having a great day. I would love to chat with you and see if we can find something that neither of us has done yet

Jul 27 1:34 AM

Yeah truth is I'd love to chat with you and I have no game so here's to maybe you throw me a bone and chat with me for a bit

Jul 27 1:36 AM

I'm going to give you a bit of advice you can take it or leave it. Before talking to an African American person on this site, take down your Afro wig pic. I don't even want to know why you had them on or how you thought that was a good idea. I don't say it hate, it's just a really bad pic and sends the wrong message.

Jul 27 5:33 /

*i don't say it WITH hate.

This man has a picture of him and some kid wearing afro wigs together. We will never know why. We will never know what they were doing or who they were pretending to be. We will never know if they put on an afro wig and shouted, "Look! I look ridiculous in this hair!" or "This beautiful hair fills me with respect for the Black community." It's just information we don't have. What we do know is this took two perfectly good afro wigs away from someone who could've really rocked them.

> Ok I went to Chambridge MD PhD really.

Sep 29 6:37 PM

> I try to keep that a secret as I want a wife lol!

Sep 29 6:37 PM

> Why would that keep you from getting a wife?

Sep 29 6:3{

> All my friends are married. Smh

Sep 29 6:38 PM

> I don't know, it seems to me that black women want a lowlife as a man.

This all seems fine until the last line: "Black women want a low-life as a man." Frigging shock of the century right there. You see, I'm a Black woman and on my list of must-haves in a guy you will not find "Hates work, loves to stab." I also know a lot of other Black women who feel the same. But hey, maybe he knows something I don't.

Hello beautiful

Mar 17 5:49 PM

You do realize you have to pictures with a confederate flag on them please look up what that history means to black people and you should probably take it off of your profile

Mar 17 6:06 PM

Okay I'll do that sorry

Mar 17 6:18 PM

So does that mean you don't want to meet up and hang out

Mar 17 6:18 PM

Okay I went and deleted the pictures

Mar 17 6:20 PM

Here's one of my favorites: This man thinks that deleting pictures of a confederate flag hanging in his house is gonna make Lacey see him as someone she wants to get to know. Sure, he took the pictures down, but are these flags still hanging in his house? Was that even his house? These are the questions no one wants answered! Can you imagine? "Well, he *did* have a confederate flag in his profile pictures, but when he took it down, I knew he was the one for me."

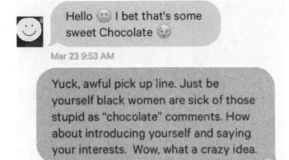

Hello 😊 I bet that's some sweet Chocolate 😏

Mar 23 9:53 AM

Yuck, awful pick up line. Just be yourself black women are sick of those stupid as "chocolate" comments. How about introducing yourself and saying your interests. Wow, what a crazy idea.

(To the tune of *Beauty and the Beast*)

🎵OLDEST PICKUP LINE
TRITE AS IT CAN BEEEE
SUPER TOP-OF-MIND
SAY "CHOCOLATE" ONE MORE TIME
I'LL GO ON A KILLING SPREEEEE!🎵

I'm drinking red tonight, I still have cab.

Sep 18 5:33 PM

Ha. I remember it, didn't know if you had a preference. I can't drink white to save my life. I guess I've always preferred darker features, even with wine 😉

"I guess I've always preferred darker features. Even with wine."
Blarf.

For starter you are absolutely amazing.. I have something to ask you, it's pretty upfront... I was wondering if by chance you were in to white men? I've never had the opportunity to have me a taste of a black woman.. And for over a year now I've had this fascination and unstoppable urge to have me some chocolate... I know I'm older than you, but I promise I can keep up with your young sexy ass... Abd who knows you might even enjoy it yourself... I need to be broke in...You could be my first... And honestly with it being my first time I'd like it to be a thin, sexy, young black woman like yourself...

This book isn't supposed to be rated R, but let me just say, WHAT? How is this man's hitting on a person basically saying, "You can have sex with me and I'm not going to be particularly good at it and you can do all the work!" This is the message that made Lacey give up completely. As you can see, she didn't have the energy to respond. She had to walk away. Just like we will now—from this section!

THE TALE OF POCAHONTAS

Halloween is that special time of year when every Black person decides whether or not they're going to have a conversation with white people about dressing up as other ethnicities. For whatever reason—call it feeling generous, or having a short-term memory—Lacey is talking to a coworker about how it's not okay to dress up as other races for Halloween. This coworker cannot stand it. She can understand why blackface is wrong (small victories), but she cannot understand why she shouldn't dress up as other ethnicities, having the ethnicity itself be the costume. So this lady starts naming different costumes, certain that Lacey will tell her one is okay.

"Indian chief?" No. And you shouldn't be saying "Indian chief." "China doll?" Not exactly sure what you mean by that, but if you mean dressing up in traditional Chinese clothes and calling yourself a doll? No. "Pocahontas?" What? "The Indian chief, Pocahontas!" Everything is wrong with what you just said. Please try to get used to never referring to America's indigenous people as "Indians." And no, definitely not. That's the worst. No Pocahontas. All of these are examples of cultural appropriation. It's not okay in your day-to-day life, and just because it's Halloween doesn't make it okay then. I'm honestly shocked you can't see that that's offensive. The lady looks down at the table and gives it a good think. She's taken in a lot of information. Maybe she just needs time. There is a long pause before the lady says, "Even Pocahontas?"

This lady is saddened. Lacey has ruined her day. But she's already opened up this can of worms, so she might as well see how far she can fling them.

So the lady calls a coworker, Roxanne, into the room. Roxanne is white but Lacey knows some of her friends are activists in the community. This lady is about to get schooled. She explains to Roxanne that all this is an overreaction. "Lacey says that people aren't supposed to dress up as other ethnicities! Not even on Halloween!" Roxanne tries to make the lady see things from Lacey's point of view. It does not work. "I just don't see why it's so bad." Roxanne has had enough of this lady. She simply says, "I can see why that's offensive and I can also see why you won't change your mind." Big fucking help. Get the fuck outta here, Roxanne. Lacey said that to Roxanne using her eyes. Then, using her mouth, she said to the lady, "Listen. It's not my job to tell people what is racist. Dressing up as different ethnicities is cultural appropriation. Whether you know it is or not." Lacey now sees that this woman is on the verge of a frigging break-down. "Soooo you're telling me it's wrong if my child dresses up as Pocahontas for Halloween?" There we go. We found it. This woman's problem was that she dressed her child up as Pocohontas for Halloween and didn't want to feel guilty about it. Too bad. Lacey tells her, "Have you read the true story of Pocahontas? If you did, you wouldn't want your baby to dress like her. That Disney version is not how it went down."

"But celebrating Indian chiefs is a nice thing to do!"

"Please stop saying 'Indian chiefs.'"

There was a long pause. It had been a good ten minutes of yapping back and forth. Yards had been gained and lost. But Lacey had made some good points without the help of the ever-useless middle-of-the-road-ing, more-harm-than-good-ing of stupid Roxanne. The lady looked up at Lacey with genuine sorrow in her eyes and said, "I think I get it....Is it okay if I dress up my child as a Native American?"

Lacey gave all the way up in many different ways that day.

Amber and I texted back and forth about this all day. Amber replied: "Sure, she can dress her child up as Pocahontas, but not if you ever want her to run for office."

LACEY'S MAGIC TRICK

Lacey once had a retail job at a high-end boutique. Because it was a bunch of rich people day in and day out, it was not uncommon to hear someone say something insane. Bosses, coworkers, and, most of all, customers. On this particular day, an older white man walks in and Lacey greets him. They talk about how he is enjoying his day. He then asks Lacey how she is. As she is talking, a stunned look comes over his face. Lacey thinks to herself, *Hmm. You know what, this old man is right. I'm an enthralling storyteller. More people should react like this when I speak.* Mid-reply, this old man cuts her off, stunned. He says, "Wow! Your diction is perfect!" It figures that an ounce of confidence would be blown into oblivion. "Where are you from?" I'm from right here in Omaha, sir. "Wow. I've just never heard a Black person speak as well as you." Now, this man is as old as time and Lacey is at work. This comment's gonna have to slide. As Lacey hurries away from him to leave him alone to let him shop, his wife walks by the store. He shouts to her. "COME IN HERE! YOU NEED TO HEAR THIS!" He motions to his wife to come in the store so she can hear Lacey talk.

Sorry, I wrote that last sentence incorrectly. He motions to his wife to come in the store so that Lacey, the carnival attraction, could impress some relic by sounding different than the two Black people he once talked to in 1948.

Lacey did not want to participate in this. She goes, "I need to make an important phone call." She walks away. The man and his wife stay there and watch her. WAITING FOR HER TO COME BACK AND WOW THEM! So Lacey picks up the phone and calls herself. As they watch her, she proceeds to leave herself the longest message. She gives a few addresses, checks up on the status of several accounts, and receives bad news about a loved one. These people are still there! Lacey babbles on and they finally leave. Those two old people were probably shocked that she figured out how to use the phone.

GETTING FOLLOWED AROUND BY JCPENNEY SECURITY: A RETROSPECTIVE

There's Tom and Jerry. Sonic and Robotnik, Sherlock and Moriarty, and Lacey and JCPenney. Let me tell you a Ruffin family classic. We are having a day at the mall and it's very fun. I'm walking around with Lacey and Mom and our brother, Jimmy, shopping for a swimsuit to wear on vacation. I'm a kid and Lacey is an old teenager. We are in JCPenney. Now, we aren't going to go blasting brand names all over the place. That's not what this is about. But if you've been followed around by loss prevention in a particular store enough to make it a whole part of a book, I think it's okay. They're so famous in my family that we changed their old jingle from "JCPenney! Doing it right!" to

"JCPenney! Up against the wall and spread 'em!" To be clear, these few times are a fraction of the times we were followed around in this store. Look! Here's a graph.

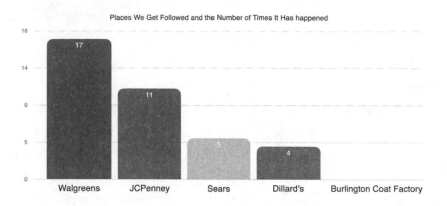

Places We Get Followed and the Number of Times It Has happened

No one has ever looked twice at me in a T.J. Maxx. I don't shoplift but I could have robbed them BLIND. And, yes, the most is that big national drugstore, but that's a whole different thing. There isn't a Black person alive who wasn't followed around at big national drugstore. Like, JCPenney may be a special Ruffin thing, but big national drugstore is all of us.

Quick story within a story: Our sister Angie was so fed up with getting followed around big national drugstore that her junior high school friends would go there with their one white friend. They'd enter separately and the Black girls would go up and down a lot of the aisles and be followed by security around the store. Meanwhile, the white friend would come in, unnoticed, and take a ton of stuff. She learned how to Make Racism Work for You! (tm) Notice how we don't use their name but do use JCPenney's name? That's how bad they were.

Okay, so we are in the girls' section at JC-fucking-Penney

as Mom is finishing up with Jimmy in the boys' section. We are looking at swimsuits when Lacey is approached by a guy who looks like a teenager with a shopping bag, a long ponytail, tan polo with khakis, and a walkie-talkie on his belt. He comes up to Lacey and is like, "JCPenney Security—come with me!"

Now, I'm frigging terrified. Mom isn't there and this man is trying to get us to go with him to a second location! And I've evolved since, but the first thought of ten-year-old me when I see this guy is *He's a white man with a ponytail! He's gonna kill us!* At this point, Lacey has not tried on a single thing. She is in a spaghetti-strap dress and is carrying a tiny purse. She hands him the purse and says, "I haven't stolen anything. Here, look for yourself." He says, "No. You need to come with me."

Ah, the joys of your first time being stopped by loss prevention. It's how you know you've become a woman. A Black woman.

Lacey's being a shoplifter sure comes as a surprise to me because I know her and she would rather lose an eye than break the rules. And not only does neither of us have the ability to shoplift, but if Mom ever thought we were shoplifting, we would have to straight-up find a new family. She would explain that her love for you was purely biological at this point and throw you into the sea. If you made it to shore safely, you could live, but not with her. It is at this point that Mom walks up and things really get fun.

Quick few facts about my mommy: She skipped second and seventh grades 'cause she has a bad case of the smarts; if you think you could win an argument with her you must be insane; and, last, she isn't fond of people messing with her children.

Mom loudly says, "What's going on?" and grabs Ponytail by

the arm. It is at this point our genius brother, Jimmy, takes the keys to the van and says, "I'll be in the car." He knew what was coming. Lacey told Mom, "He thinks I stole something and wants me to go with him." My mother says that's not happening.

"Your daughter was shoplifting. We saw her on the security cameras."

"Oh! You watched her shoplift? I'd love to see that footage, as I have been with her all day."

"We can't show that to you."

"I bet you can't. Do you have any proof she was shoplifting?"

"The dress she is wearing still has a tag on it."

"So you didn't see her shoplifting at all. You saw the dress she is wearing still had a tag on it. You saw a white price tag on the inside of a white dress on security footage. You must have state-of-the-art cameras."

(It is in this exact moment that he realizes he's been tripped up in his own words.)

At this point shoppers have started to gather. This is before Worldstar and social media. The only way to catch a glimpse of real humiliation was to just so happen to be there. These folks were lucky. They got to watch a real-life shoplifter get caught! Lacey is embarrassed to death and convinces Mom to let her go with them so this doesn't escalate any further. We follow Ponytail to the shoe department. He knocks a special secret knock on what I would have assumed was a wall. It swings open and Lacey and this guy go inside.

Inside, there are a bunch of fools looking at security camera feeds. Lacey walks in and they ask her to turn around and lift up her hair. "Why? I'm not getting undressed." There is not much that can fit under this dress. He explains, "No, the employee at the register saw a tag." Lacey turns around and there is a small piece of plastic that you would see on a new item still attached to her dress. One of the men says, "It's not our tag." Lacey replies, "You humiliated me and marched me through your department store over a piece of plastic? I'm going to need your names." They all refuse to tell her any names and send Lacey out of the room back to us.

When Lacey comes out, she tells Mom that she was unable to get their names. Mom shouts to their secret door, reminding them they are terrible at their jobs. To us, she is defending Lacey's honor. To passersby, she is yelling at a wall. The best part of it was when he went back into the room, he knocked a special knock and slid into the office. Mom, while yelling, knocked the *exact* special knock and shouted, "I know about your little secret knock. You're not slick."

To this day, I say that to myself every time I knock on a door.

Lacey looked into suing them and was told by a lawyer that since she went with them willingly to look at the tag, not much could be done. He told her, "If something like that happens again, just walk away."

It was really important for us to see Mom handle this situation this way. I think a lot of people think there's no way they can protest how they're being treated. But this was how I learned you can. And, again, I'll do whatever I want to do whenever I want to do it, but it's nice to know that if I feel like it, I can really show the fuck out and that's okay too. I have options.

After that incident, Lacey would see Ponytail every single time she was there. He would follow her around whenever she was in the store and Lacey would say, "I see you! I see what you're doing." He must stop every Black person who comes in there, so he doesn't remember Lacey. But Lacey remembers him because in order to go into the store, she has to consider if she can stand being followed around or not. He would essentially harass her.

Almost a year to the day later, Lacey was seeing *The Lion King* at the same mall. The movie theater was right next to JCPenney. The setup goes: JCPenney, mall bathrooms, movie theater, exit to the mall. Lacey and her boyfriend are talking about how much fun they just had. He decides to go to the bathroom. Lacey waits for him right outside. The movie had just ended and the whole theater full of people had emptied out and everyone was walking to the exit. As Lacey's standing there waiting, she hears someone yell, "JCPenney Security! Ma'am, come with me!" Now, since Lacey's many run-ins with them, everyone she knows teases her by yelling "Stop! JCPenney Security!" to her while in public. It's funny. So when she's in the mall surrounded by people, she assumes this is being yelled by a friend of hers. She feels a hand grab her arm. A voice says, "Where are those bags you just had?" Whichever friend of hers this is is really committed. She turns around and it's Ponytail.

Welp, you know what they say: "When you find a job you stink at, do it until you ruin lives."

Somehow, in the sea of people, he found her and accused her of stealing. Terrible as it is, it's nice to know you're some-one's favorite. Looking for shoplifters, settling for Lacey, her turning out to be innocent, and then starting all over again—it's the 🎵 CIIIRCLE OF LIIIIFE 🎵! She pulls out of his grip and says, "This is *not* happening again." Ponytail really begins to make a scene here in the mall in the middle of this sea of people. "Don't you go anywhere! We're taking you in!" Lacey calmly walks into the men's bathroom to get her boyfriend. She doesn't care. It's time to go. Ponytail yells, "Stop! Come back here." Her boyfriend is at the urinal and Lacey yells, "JCP did it again! This guy just grabbed my arm and accused me of stealing." Boyfriend finishes peeing and they come out of the restroom. "But you weren't even *in* JCPenney today!" Ponytail is trying to block the restroom exit while yelling into a walkie-talkie. "Yes, I have her right here. Hurry up!" They push past him and start walking to the exit. This is what the lawyer told them to do. As they make their way to the exit, two more security guys show up. Ponytail points at Lacey and says, "She's right here!" At this point, people have stopped leaving the mall and are crowded around Lacey, her boyfriend, and the now three security guards. They don't stop walking to the exit. Security is closing in. Boyfriend makes sure to yell, "You better not touch her!" As they close in on the exit, the three security guards block their path. They're going to grab them. Here we go. Right before they do, a fourth security guard runs up to them and says to his colleagues, "What are you doing? That's not her!"

The rest of them, without apology, turn and just walk away. Not a word. There is a huge crowd watching and they say nothing. Lacey is pissed. All of that humiliation for no reason at all. She says, "That's it? You guys are going to stalk me, chase me, accuse me of stealing, and then just walk away? I need to speak to a supervisor!" She follows them into JCPenney. They're far ahead, but she can see them leading a girl with her hands cuffed behind her. They've found the culprit, and you will never believe what she looks like. She's Hispanic, 200 pounds, and has mustard-yellow bell-bottoms on. Lacey has on a summer dress. You couldn't find a pair of mustard-yellow bell-bottoms? That's all you had to say! If you ever have seen mustard-yellow bell-bottoms, you frigging remember that shit! These idiots can't even say "yellow pants"? It's like the description they gave was "girl" when it should've been "girl riding a unicorn."

At this time, mall security comes up and says, "It's best if you leave." Even though they took nothing, they still got kicked out of the mall. Infuriatingly believable. They walk out the mall entrance, turn the corner, and walk right back in the JCPenney entrance. They think they've taken this girl to a secret room, but it's no secret to Lacey. Lacey marches right down to the shoe department and knocks the secret knock on the secret door that looks like a wall. The very knock we have been doing and laughing about for the past year. As soon as she does, the door swings all the way open. She sees the entire security staff sitting there. Everyone turns to look at her, a-frigging-ghast. The shocked look on their faces is priceless. Lacey launches into her tirade.

"Do you know how I know this door is here? Do you know how I know your little secret knock? Because you bag of ass-holes did this to me last year. You spend all your days in this cave finding people to harass. And I know that's what you're doing because if you were concerned with stopping theft, I wouldn't have had this many run-ins with you after never having stolen in my entire life. It has to be on purpose because you couldn't be this bad at your jobs. If you're going to continue to conduct yourselves like JCPenney is the Wild West, I'm going to need some names." Everyone refused to give their name except the supervisor.

This time the good lawyer was unavailable, so she ended up with a horrible lawyer. JCP admitted no wrongdoing and offered a fifty-dollar gift certificate. The opportunity to shop and be watched like a hawk by a bunch of cave dwellers? Sigh. There was once a news piece about how a lady who was stopped and searched in a store in front of everyone got a million dollars. Doing the math, I think they owe Lacey fifty eleven billiondy dollars.

The point of those stories is: JCPenney had some of the best sales in all of retail. It's so good that we know this is gonna happen and we still go. I can remember being followed around in more than one JCPenney. Their clearance is, like, Kohl's-level good. I would do almost anything for a four-dollar shirt. And before you say "You shouldn't give them your business," let me just say, "FOUR-DOLLAR SHIRTS."

I Find This Hard to Believe

This is a collection of stories that Lacey can tell her friends or people who know her well. They are certainly not impossible to believe, but they do sound like a fun lie. This shit would not fly with strangers. You would think she's lying. She is not. We are gonna move a little more into the stories where there is a real disconnect. A lot of these stories will highlight what is likely to happen to you when you're the only Black person someone has come in contact with.

And, as you read this book, you should know my life is great. Aside from my shitty jobs, I have a happy life with great friends and a great family. It's just that, every Monday, Tuesday, Wednesday, Thursday, and Friday, someone says something insane to me.

YOU'RE WRONG ABOUT THE BLACK EXPERIENCE. LET ME, A WHITE, TELL YOU ABOUT IT

So, there's this thing you may or may not be aware of. When people who don't normally talk to Black people end up talking to Black people, they usually do one of three things: talk to you about "Black stuff," which is anything from actual Black stuff to "I like Savion Glover. Do you?" Or they tell you about a Black person they know. "I have this friend, Marcus, who…" Lots of times, they talk to you like that because it feels good to have had a good interaction with a Black person. I think it makes them feel like they're not racist. Whatever the reason, they seem to enjoy it. But, lastly, there is the kind of person in this category who meets a Black person and is immediately mad and rude. Never in front of another white person who isn't their child or wife, but under the right circumstances, these people will talk to you like it's 1909. I have a theory about why this happens. Now, I don't know if this is true or not, but I think that the last category of white person sees Black people shopping at the same store, having a mutual friend, or just sharing a sidewalk. And it makes them realize we are the same. And once they lose their perceived upper hand, they fucking freak out. Humans need joy to live. Most people's joy comes from friends and family, or from hobbies and work, but some people's joy comes from the idea that they are superior. So my living a life that is better than theirs destroys their joy. They rage against the idea that they ain't shit. It's like if someone walked up to me and said, "You can't pull off high-waisted slacks and a crop top." It would change my very idea of myself. And I would hurt their feelings so bad. I would wreck them. Simply wreck them. And they would deserve it.

We say all that to say that, sometimes, people see a Black person and panic and just say the first thing that comes to mind. Lacey had just met a white coworker and she was like, "Why is she talking to me?" Then the coworker told her that she had a Black fiancé and Lacey was like, "Oh. That's why she's talking to me." She said she was jealous of our skin because it was always smooth and soft. "I just love the feel of your skin. I constantly have to apply lotion to my skin or it just gets so dry." Where did she learn that Black people's skin comes naturally moisturized? Does she not know the opposite is the stereotype? Has she never heard of ashiness? Or did she— and this is the most likely—see two Black people who had a lot of cocoa butter on and assume it was natural? Whatever the reason, it's cool that she thinks that. When she said this, Lacey just let her think it. We'd like to encourage everyone to Start Fun Black Stereotypes (tm)!

At this same job, Lacey was talking to a coworker and mentioned how someone had mistaken her for a director who worked in another building. Of course they mistook her for her; she was the only other Black lady at work. Luckily, Lacey was here first. 'Cause one of us is getting called the other one's name. You may not know this, but, in many cases, nothing is harder than adding the name of a second Black person to a white person's mind. I was the second Black actress at my theater and I still respond to the name Holly.

My friend told me a story about how when he was three years old, there was only one Black family in the neighborhood, the Johnsons. And whenever he saw Black people in the supermarket, he'd point at them and shout, "Look, it's the Johnsons!" His family would be embarrassed and apologize. But he was three! Grown men and women do that every single day. They assume you're related to the other Black person they know. Someone somewhere is doing it right now! When people say to me, "You know who you look like?"

I'm always livid 'til they finish their sentence with "Lacey Lamar."

Aww.

They actually say I look like "a young Lacey Lamar."

People tell me "You look like what Amber Ruffin would look like if she was cute."

Shut up.

Anyhoo, the coworker had never met this individual but she had heard them talk about the lady Lacey is always mistaken for and how she had a bubbly and upbeat personality. She then said, "That director is Black? Weird, I never would have thought that because normally, Black women are serious all the time."

Did you feel that? In one sentence we completely understood who this woman is. We have no way of knowing this, but I believe we all just pictured the exact same woman. Let me check. Lacey, is this woman the type of person who says things like, "Mic drop," "Thank you for coming to my TED Talk," "I'm one hundred percent that bitch," and stuff like that, but like, dead serious and years too late?

Yes.

And, does she have one of those faces where it looks like one of her eyebrows is raised in disgust all the time? But it's not, that's just her face?

Yes.

Okay. That was a fun experiment.

Stories about white people getting Black stereotypes wrong are confusing. It's like, "How did you come to that conclusion? But also, it feels refreshing not to hear the same five stereotypes over and over. SO I'M CONFLICTED. Like this one: It was Lacey's birthday and she was juuuust getting lulled into a false sense of security by her coworkers. It had been a while since any real racist event. And the number of high-level racists was really down to only one. Ellen. Everyone was fine, but Ellen was like, "Do you *like* having hair like that? You guys think it's fun and not gross, right?" Just the worst of the worst. Out-loud ignorant and kind of proud of it and full of dumb questions. But other than her, things were great! They were even giving Lacey a birthday potluck! Each of her coworkers brought something and made a pretty nice spread! Lacey was determined to have fun even though Ellen was there. One bad apple isn't going to spoil this bunch. Besides, it's Lacey's birthday! Plus, they worked hard to do something nice for her. Excited, Lacey thanked them and grabbed a plate and got to eatin'! As she was putting food on her plate, her least-favorite coworker, Ellen, yelled out, "Oh my god! She *did* choose the salad!" Lacey stared at her, bewildered. Ellen then explained that as they were planning the potluck, there was a discussion about whether they should even bring salad because she didn't think Black people ate it. She had "never seen a Black person eat salad before." Okay. This is the behavior we all expected, and Ellen at her worst can't stop the fun. Lacey was like, "Ellen, that is a crazy thing to say." But she looked around and most of her other co-workers were nodding their heads in agreement. They didn't think Black people ate salad. They didn't think Black people ate SALAD. Salad. Sal. Ad. It made Lacey a little sad but it also was a harsh reminder not to get too comfortable at work.

Another head-scratcher: Lacey was at a meeting at work and at the time there was a very high-profile missing-persons case involving a white woman. Someone brought up the case at the meeting and talked about how women aren't safe any-where anymore. Lacey agreed, and a white woman at the meeting said, "Lacey, *you're* safe, no one is going to try to mess with a Black woman." You already know Lacey was the only Black person in the room. She told them Black women go missing all the time. Her boss rolled her eyes and said, "Black women get kidnapped?" and everyone laughed. In that moment, Lacey prayed to be kidnapped but no one came.

TRYING TO WIN OVER HER RACIST ART TEACHER: AN IMPOSSIBILITY

Lacey was in the fifth grade when she met a teacher who would help her better understand racist people. Well, not really *understand* them as much as *be able to see them coming*. Okay, so Lacey was always great at art. She has always been able to draw really well and, if it's possible, we are going to put some of her little-kid art right here:

Yes, that is a picture of El DeBarge. It was drawn when Lacey was eight years old. Yes, he is worth googling. Yes, Lacey wanted to marry him. Yes, she still wants to marry him. El, please be in contact. So Lacey was in fifth grade and it was time for their first art class. Lacey was thrilled because, earlier that week, she had just drawn her most beautiful work to date: a life-sized pastel portrait of Leif Erikson. No, he's not worth googling.

For a book report, Lacey had to draw a picture of a famous

person. She chose Leif Erikson because we had a book about him in the house. (Mom and Dad went to the book auction down the street once a month and would buy big bunches of books. You never knew what you were gonna get and it's why we all have at least one random hobby. Belly dancing, mosaics, sign language. We had books about everything. And they also had all kinds of art supplies because they used to have a day-care center. A kid's dream place to grow up, really.) So Lacey, instead of drawing a regular-sized picture like every other child did, drew a giant, life-sized pastel of Leif Erikson. She worked on it all weekend and knew it was the pinnacle of her life's work. She had never felt pride like this. It was so stunning that the teacher entered it into an art contest at Omaha's art museum downtown and it got first place. Everyone was so proud that the teacher put the drawing on display for them to look at every day next to the chalkboard.

In walks their new art teacher, who we will call Mrs. Art. Now, Mrs. Art was a big old meanie. She was short, stubby, and had what I'm pretty sure was a severely permed mullet. She wore moccasins and long beaded necklaces. She seemed like a hippie. If you were judging her based on her looks, you would think, *This lady has been to a sit-in or two; she knows what's up*. But her behavior did not match her exterior. This woman was hateful.

Mrs. Art greets the class and walks right up to the chalk-board. Lacey is thrilled. She's going to see it! She's gonna see Lacey's beautiful drawing she worked so hard on! Mrs. Art writes her name on the board and just so happens to look Leif Erikson right in the eye. She walks over to him and turns to the class.

Did your teacher draw this?

No. I did.

That's a lie. There's no way you drew this.

She grabs the life-sized portrait of Leif Erikson off the wall. She looks Lacey in the eye as she rips it in half in one long motion from his head down to his crotch. She crumples up the two halves and throws the whole thing in the trash. In a silent rage, Lacey gets up and walks out of the classroom, past the principal's office, past the secretary, and right out of the school. No one stops her because she is such a goodie-goodie A-plus student. She walks down the street in shock, crying her eyes out. She gets home sometime between eleven o'clock and noon. She remembers that little detail because mom was watching *The Young and the Restless*. She comes in the door and Mom turns around and asks, "What are you doing here?" Lacey explains what happened. Mom takes her right back up to school. At this point, Lacey has been gone for thirty minutes.

Mom has a meeting with the principal and Mrs. Art. Who knows what was said in this meeting, but Mrs. Art comes out and gives Lacey an apology.

But instead of feeling discouraged, she thought, *Maybe I can win this lady over if I just work hard enough. After all, she's the art teacher and I love art. We* have *to get along!* This is one of the first times the way someone looks does not match up with how they behave. It's a pivotal moment in Lacey's life because if you couldn't judge people based on what they look like, her racism spidey sense would have to develop. And develop it did! She didn't know this then, but Mrs. Art was one of those "women are the n*****s of the world" type of people who want so desperately for white women's suffering to outweigh the suffering of Black people. You know—one of those.

Throughout the school year, Mrs. Art says all kinds of doozies. She would call Black students "colored" or "negro." Now, Lacey was a bit young to know that if you use these words, you're for certain a piece of shit. But she soon figured it out. Mrs. Art treated the white students one way and the Black students another. It all came to a head during an art project called Animals from Africa. Mrs. Art showed her true colors when she told the class that slavery was not as bad as it seemed. It made white people look bad, but having slaves was nothing but peer pressure. "If your neighbor had slaves, why wouldn't you want to have some, too?" She said that to a room full of fifth-grade Black and white children. This woman called slavery a result of peer pressure. Is this what white people think? Wait. Don't answer that. I don't ever want the answer to that question. Lacey knew then that it was okay not only never to get this woman's approval, but also to dislike her.

Many years later, Lacey was working at a retirement home. Usually, residents have visitors weekly or monthly. Many times they make friends with other residents. But sometimes they don't have visitors or make any friends. One day, Lacey is walking through the common area and finds an old lady who is alone and confused. Lacey decides to talk to her.

"Hi! How are you today?" As she looks at her, the woman doesn't respond. She's just staring off into space. Lacey realizes she's talking to Mrs. Art. Over the months while she's there she's rude to the staff and mostly confused, but what strikes Lacey is that she never sees her make friends with any of the residents or have any visitors. No one ever comes to visit her and, to make things even worse, she dies alone. This mean old lady who was pretty darn horrible seems to get her comeuppance. It doesn't feel good. It's not even what fifth-grade Lacey would have wished for her. It's simply a case of bad things happening to bad people.

QUOTES FROM THE WHITE LADY AT WORK WHO HATES LACEY FOR NO REASON[1]

At her corporate job, Lacey once had a coworker who was nice to everyone but her. She had a very fun disorder that made her immediately say the opposite of whatever Lacey had just said. Each time, she refuted Lacey's statements loudly, proudly, and with a little bit of snark. Eventually Lacey started to write down all the instances because of the level of amusement it brought her.

Everyone having a fun lunchtime conversation about their favorite holidays:

Lacey: I love Christmas.

Lady: I hate Christmas; it's just Jesus's birthday. Why all the gifts?

This lady would always talk about bringing people to her Zumba class with her:

Lacey: I do some personal training. I'm always in the gym exercising.

Lady: I hate exercising.

---

1 We know the reason.

Midwinter on a twenty-degree day:

Lacey: It's cold outside.

Lady: It's not cold. It's not cold right now.

Other People in the Room: Yes, it is cold.

Lacey: Well at least when it's cold, you can get warm with layers.

Lady: I hate layers.

Lacey: I like chocolate.

Lady: I hate sweets! I do not eat desserts. I mean, maybe sometimes. But just, like, key lime pie, banana cream pie, root-beer floats, whipped cream, fruit pie, glazed doughnuts, blueberry cake doughnuts, and cheesecake. But normally I don't like desserts.

That is exactly what she said. Lacey wrote it down word for word. It is a complete list of sweets. She does not hate any sweets. Her list of sweets that she likes is a complete list of sweets that exist.

A man delivered a package. It was very important. No one could find it. They asked Lacey who the delivery guy was. "There's only two people who deliver here. Was he the old guy or the young guy?" The lady is not a part of this conversation. She is chiming in from across the room.

Them: Is he the old guy or the young guy?

Lacey: Oh, he had to be the old guy.

Lady: I wouldn't call him old.

Lacey: Okay. Well, he was sixty-plus.

Lady: That's not old.

Lacey: Can I say anything that you would agree with? Anything I say, you disagree with. Is there anything I could say that you would agree with?

The lady walked away. She did not care for Lacey's attitude. This day, it was smart of her to walk away.

It's just Lacey and the lady in a room waiting for a meeting to start.

Lacey: Good morning!

Lady: ...

(After six minutes of sitting in silence)

Lady: I'm not talking to you. But it's because I don't talk to anyone.

There was a news story about an Uber driver kidnapping a woman.

Lady: Did you see that Black guy kidnapping women from his Uber? If I saw that Black guy, I would have never gotten in his car.

So this woman has never had a Black Uber driver? What happens if she calls one? She just doesn't get in? She eats the five-dollar cancellation fee and just takes the next one? I have had a grand total of four white Uber drivers in my *life*, so good luck.

PORTRAIT OF AN HR WOMAN WHO IS A FULL PIECE OF SHIT

What would happen if the HR woman at Lacey's office made racist comments day in and day out? Nothing!

This woman, let's call her Nancy, was the bane of Lacey's existence. Here's how she got hired. Early in this job, Lacey was in the meeting when they were hiring an HR person. There were two candidates, Nancy and a perfect man who was overqualified. He talked about different situations and how he would resolve issues of sexism and racism. He was so smart and sharp, it never occurred to Lacey he wouldn't be hired. Instead, they hired the woman who was a little dumb and boring. Lacey asked a coworker why the guy she liked didn't get hired. "Oh, you mean the gay one?" Aaaaand there you have your answer. But really, it makes no sense that she was hired. And to make sure you get how insane the decision to pay this woman to be around other people was, we are going to tell you nine stories about her. We have given each story a title that, while it makes no sense, makes more sense than her being hired.

Story One: Sudoku Fun

At this terrible job, when someone is hired, you take them out for lunch. So they all took Nancy out to a restaurant. That sounds fun because, hey, free food. But going to a restaurant with shitty people from your job is unpleasant at best. Because at work, when someone says something crazy, you can just walk away. But being stuck in a booth with all of the higher-ups is much more tricky. Now, at this job, the more money you make, the more racist you are. That may be the case at a lot of jobs. You know what? I'm gonna go ahead and say that is likely the case at most jobs. At this particular dinner, it was Lacey, Nancy, and folks from corporate. Racist, racist corporate.

Here's how the conversation went. Everyone says what kind of food they like. Everyone names different kinds of food. Someone says, Indian food. Nancy goes, "I hate Indian food. I can't stand the smell of it." Now, I don't know if you can see where this is going immediately, but Lacey can. The very next thing this idiot says is "Indians are dirty." So Lacey responds, "Oh! How are Indians dirty?" Nancy replies, "Well, I had an Indian neighbor who had the worst lawn."

Lacey: And tell me how that's dirty.

Nancy: He didn't know how to mow it.

Lacey: Tell me how that's dirty.

Nancy: Well, he tried to mow his lawn and his lawn mower would go 'round and 'round and finally my husband had to help him.

Lacey: So? I don't know how to use the lawn mower. I hire someone to mow my lawn. Am I dirty?

Nancy: No.

Lacey: Did he learn how to use the mower?

Nancy: Yes.

Lacey: Well then, your story makes no sense. If not understanding how to use your lawn mower and then becoming good at it means you're dirty, all of us are dirty.

The topic abruptly changed to burgers.

This was the beginning of the opposite of a beautiful friendship. Here are just a few fun stories from Nancy, a real-life HR person who worked at a real company in the 2010s. THE LATE 2010s. IN AMERICA.

Story Two: Zoobamafoo!

Nancy came into Lacey's office while Lacey was having a lovely conversation with a white colleague of theirs.

Lovely is a strong word. How about *fine*?

50

They were having a fine talk when Nancy barged in on their conversation to start a conversation about Trump. And not with Lacey, the person whose office it was, but with the white person Lacey was talking to. To be clear, she came into Lacey's office and started a conversation with the person Lacey was talking to. The person whose office it wasn't. She said, "Thank god Trump is building that wall because we are letting in all the ants." This woman came into Lacey's office to talk about Mexican people being "ants." It wouldn't be long before Lacey was fired. Lacey knew exactly who this lady was. She's kind of hard to explain. Nancy was a solid racist with hints of "getting off on treating minorities poorly" and overtones of "seeking out minorities to shit on them." She just wants to feel superior. So enduring this job would be the classic game of "Try to stay on this side of whipping boy." Lacey will stay here and look for another job while she prepares to lose this job.

Story Three: A Can of Pee

Nancy would greet everyone in the room in every meeting. Except for Lacey and Cindy, the Hispanic lady who worked there. The ten other people in the room were each greeted by name. This happened every day.

Story Four: Jersey Shore

Nancy has trouble telling Black employees apart. It's as jarring as it is hilarious. She gets people's names wrong a lot. Whenever this happens I always think, *How is this person functioning in the world?* Like, when they watch TV, do they think, *Why does Barack Obama host* Family Feud?

Story Five: A Big Beehive

They're on a conference call with a lady from corporate HR. They're trying to get an ad put in an employment agency newsletter. Before the call starts, Nancy says, "Listen to this woman try to talk. Ugh. She is ignorant and she doesn't know what she's talking about. She's not smart enough to be in this position and, worst of all, she's fake sugary sweet. You know? You can tell she's just pretending to be nice." Lacey knew immediately she would be a Black woman. Nancy hates that this lady has a nice job. Technically, she's Nancy's boss. She can't stand it. Nancy wishes she had that job. The call begins. This woman is perfect. Superprofessional and knowledgeable. So Lacey starts asking this lady questions that Nancy should be able to answer but can't. Just to make sure Nancy knows she truly sucks a butt. It's not a nice thing to do, but it feels great!

Story Six: Now on Netflix

The Hispanic girl was always asked to go pick up lunch orders for people and serve them. This was NOT her job. But she was Hispanic, so it was. Then one day they called Lacey and said, "Cindy's sick. Can you go get food?" Lacey said, "No. That's not my job."

Story Seven: Michael Bivins[1]

They asked Cindy to ask her mom if she could babysit for them. To babysit! They don't know her mom. They just know she's Hispanic. They assume that her mom had so little going on that

---

1   If you recognized that name, give me your phone number so we can text on a regular basis.

she would love to babysit for them so they could, presumably, go out, have some drinks, and talk shit about her.

Cindy caught on very, very slowly. She warned Lacey of possible racism: "I think they're singling us out! I . . . I think we're gonna get fired!" This child was *just* discovering racism; meanwhile Lacey had already cleared out her desk.

Story Eight: Watergate

Lacey had to pick up supplies downtown and just so happened to see some Cinco de Mayo festivities! She came back to work and said how delighted she was to have gotten a glimpse of the parade. Their reply was so insane that afterward, she immediately ran to her desk to write it down:

"Going to Mexico is one thing because you're at a resort but South Omaha has those real dirty Mexicans. Now, I don't do that. You could get shot or stabbed."

This went on for a month. These people were amazingly racist every day. And every day Lacey was able to pay rent and eat food. There aren't really words to describe how immune you become to this sort of thing. The real shame here is Cindy. She doesn't even realize what's happening to her. She grew up in West Omaha. Her parents had money. I don't think they prepared her for this. Anyhoo, it was all pretty bad, but the story that got Lacey fired was:

Story Nine: Turpentine

The boss and HR made an announcement that they were getting an intern! A surprise because why would they do that when Cindy is willing to do whatever they want for them? So, like everyone who works everywhere, the boss and Nancy, who, remember, is the HR lady, take the new intern around and introduce her to everyone.

The building is a complete circle. When Lacey started, she was introduced to everyone and it was very laid-back. "You can show up in pajamas and as long as you get your work done—it's fine!" People said hi, she said hi, and they moved on to the next office.

Lacey is in her office with Cindy. They can hear the intern being introduced to everyone. It's going pretty quickly and Lacey doesn't want the girl to feel nervous. So when she comes to her office, Lacey's gonna see if she can't put the girl at ease. They introduce the intern. Lacey says: "Hi! What high school do you go to? That's great! How are you? First job? Are you excited?" Lacey asks a bunch of questions, the girl seems to chill out a bit, and they move on. Lacey talked to this child more than anyone else; she knows this is a fact, because she and Cindy heard all the intros. At least an hour later, Lacey gets a phone call from the CEO. She says, "I need you both in my office right now."

Lacey, like I bet everyone else, grabs a notebook and a pen before going into this office. She assumes they need something done. She and Cindy walk to the CEO's office. There are six people in there: the CEO, Nancy and the other boss, and three others. When they get there, the others have made sure they're sitting on big, normal chairs, but they ask Lacey and her Hispanic coworker to share a tiny children's-bench thing. It's hard to explain, but it's a piece of furniture that shouldn't be in anyone's office. It seems like it was there just to sit people on so they can talk down to them. All you need to know about this bench is it was so small their butts were touching!

So first of all, let's say you're the most fair people in the world. Can you see how maybe you should not put the only Black woman and the only Hispanic woman on a baby bench and reprimand them from your giant chairs? Do you think white people think about that?

No.

No one thinks, *Put two more chairs out?*

No, they are probably like, "Let 'em sit on the floor!" Then you accidentally found the bench. You should be grateful for the bench.

That is gross and probably true.

The CEO says, "We heard you met the intern today." Lacey thinks the intern has done something crazy. The CEO goes on to ask Lacey, "How did that go?" Lacey replies, "It went great!" The CEO turns to the Hispanic lady and says, "How did that go?" Cindy replies, "Great!" She turns to Nancy and says, "Is there something you would like to say?" Nancy turns to us and says, "First of all, you guys were very rude. I was shocked at your behavior." Now, this seems crazy, but as we have established, racists don't need a reason. We are the reason. Nancy goes on to say, "We were very disappointed that the intern was treated this way." Lacey and Cindy are left to wonder what the lie is that the CEO was told. It could be anything! They could have told the CEO that they catcalled the intern, that they told her this was a bad place to work, they could've even told the

CEO that they hit the intern! That's why the cops are here to take you to jail! The mind wanders.

What Nancy said was "You did not stand up and talk about your role in our company. You put your heads down and went back to your computers." And Nancy's crony, their boss, co-signs. As cronies are want to do. As in all meetings Lacey has ever been to, she's writing it all down. Then the boss says, "Do you need extra training? What can we do to help you guys to be polite to people? How could you have done this differently? You two need to sit here and think about that."

Bitch, I am forty-five years old.

Then everyone takes turns talking about their disappointment in them. Now, I need you to understand that an average Netflix show is forty-five minutes long, and these people spoke for forty-one minutes. Lacey and Cindy were reprimanded for forty-one minutes about a situation that did not happen. When the bosses were done, Lacey said, "That did not happen. I don't know what to tell you." The bosses were like, "The discussion is over." Defeated, Lacey went to her desk. She realized the scales had tipped so badly in favor of "whipping boy" that she would have to leave. So she might as well be heard. She grabs her notebook and goes back to the CEO's office.

Lacey comes back into the room. They are all still there. She says, "I need to say this. I was not rude and this did not happen. The fact that you so blindly believe Nancy that you would hold a whole meeting isn't surprising but disappointing." And the boss says, "We didn't say you were rude." Lacey: "It says here in my notes 'rude.' You used the word 'rude' more than once.

If we weren't rude, then why did we have this meeting with six people? I'm confused. Have you forgotten what you said?"

Boss: We were just trying to get to the bottom of this.

Lacey looks through her notes.

Lacey: The bottom of what? How you were disappointed with our behavior? Because if we weren't rude, why were you disappointed?

Boss: We never said we were disappointed.

Lacey: You did. You said it, and Nancy said it. It's right here in my notes.

Boss: Ugh, Lacey, why are you always taking notes?

Lacey: For times like this, when everyone has to have a meeting, the biggest part of which you can't remember. Also, when I was introduced to this company and walked around to everyone, no one stood up and told me their job title. And, boss, YOU were the one who took me around that day. People said hello and maybe their name. So was a meeting called with six people then? When I was taken around? No special greeting was given to me and no meeting was called. When you start at a company you do as others do. Being casual is the motto of this entire building. I know that I did nothing wrong. I was very nice. Just ask the intern. I am shocked by this whole situation. Company rules should not be made up on the spot. You sat us down like children and accused us of something that didn't happen. And then you say you're worried about us representing the company over a greeting? This has just shown me some people are more valued than others. Forty minutes' reprimand about a greeting? A greeting that you've completely backpedaled on? How much money did a forty-minute waste of eight people's time cost this company?

Lacey was made the boss of the company and was heralded a hero! Just kidding. She was fired.

And that's the end of the HR lady story. Until two years later.

Lacey is working at a different home. She hasn't seen Nancy in two years. It's your same old same old. Nothing outstandingly terrible or wonderful. But the thing is, you don't realize how good you have it until you don't. 'Cause after working there for quite some time, guess who comes sauntering in? Nancy. She doesn't recognize Lacey at all. She has no clue who Lacey is because her hair is different.

Lacey

Of course she doesn't recognize her. What is Lacey, some supersecret spy? Also, hey, FBI, wanna catch racists? Use any

Black woman and a variety of wigs. Ooh! Another idea: Want to find out who is racist at your company? Hire a Black lady, introduce her to everyone, and the very next week do it again but in a wig. If people are like, "I hate 'em both," they're racist.

After Nancy stopped having to see Lacey every day, Lacey's face moved from the "avoid her on purpose" category to "wouldn't talk to her anyway" category in her mind. Lacey is shocked but says nothing. Nancy walks right past her. She finds out Nancy is there because she is training a new HR person. Now, for those of you who don't have good memories, the worst HR person on the planet is going to train someone. All we can do is hope that this person was at least normal to begin with. And— I'll go ahead and stop the guessing now—the HR person Nancy is training is not normal. She's horrible. To the point where the white people at this job tell Lacey, "Oh my god, this new woman is so rude to Black people." The *white people* warned her. At the last job, Nancy was the second coming of terrible and those white people didn't say a word. So if this new lady was so bad that regular white people could see it, it's going to be a dark season of work. The bright side is, within a few short days of working there, this new lady has multiple complaints already. Oh, wait. She has multiple complaints against her and still has her job. That's not a bright side, that's a white side. She has been so terrible that more than one person has complained. Now, unfortunately, when you complain to HR about an HR person, oftentimes nothing gets done. Lacey is venting to an old white coworker. The coworker's advice is this: "I'm gonna tell you what I tell everyone else: Shut up and take it." Super-duper-gross advice. But not if you want to keep your job.

So it's been a few weeks at this point and Lacey has never had to look at, talk to, or deal with the new HR lady. Lacey is happily walking down the hallway when she sees one of her favorite coworkers in a hurry. "Hey, Lacey, could you do me a favor and drop this folder off for me?" "Of course!" Lacey grabs the folder from her without thinking. She looks at it and realizes it needs to be delivered to HR! Dun-dun-duuuunnnn! Let's take a quick look at the options:

1. She can do the same thing to someone else. Let them run the risk of going into the HR office, which now has two actual fire-breathing dragons in it.
2. She can just leave it somewhere, hoping someone else will see it and bring it to HR. Solid, but this option could get her work friend in trouble.
3. She can suck it up.

She's got no choice. She's got to go. On her way, she thinks, *What are the odds Nancy or the new HR lady will even be in there?* Well, the answer is zero, because when she steps into the office, she sees they're *both* in there! Eggshells. Okay. You can do this. Lacey walks in and sees Nancy training the mean HR lady. Lacey hands her the folder and says, "Hello, I was told to give you this." And immediately, this new HR lady shouts, "No! No! No!" while snapping her fingers like you would at a cat on the countertop. This twenty-something white woman is reprimanding Lacey like a bad dog.

Here's why you shouldn't talk to Black people like that—just kidding. Can you imagine if I actually explained that?

Without replying at all, Lacey turns around and walks out

of the room, into their boss's office, and tells her what just happened. "She's gonna have to change her tone. Not just talking to me, but with every Black woman at the office. Someone will hurt that woman." The boss says, "This is un-professional. We will talk to her immediately." That is code for "Lacey, how dare you. You will be fired within the next month." When Lacey told her coworkers, they said, "Why would you say anything? You know you'll just get fired." You're supposed to just take it. Until you can't. Lacey can't. She got fired shortly after.

I just had a great idea! Remember the movie *9 to 5* about the women who had to put up with a lot of crap at work? There should be a remake of it where everyone is Black and they have to put up with racism. Call it *Real Life* and shoot it for free by putting a camera in almost any workplace anywhere.

And, for contrast, let me tell you a story about my job. I'm about four years into writing on *Late Night with Seth Meyers*, easily the best job I've ever had, and I love it. Every day, I fall deeper in love with each person who works on the show, and it's a blast. On a show where I get to absolutely rail against racist crap, everyone knows that if they say anything crazy, I'll let them have it. But, also, the show rails against racist crap, so if someone who hated Black people worked there, they would absolutely want to quit. This is not the place. Also, I told you before, but I have that thing where if you have been around a lot of racism, you can see racist behavior coming. Like, you know when you've met someone who is gonna say a crazy thing to you, or when you've met someone who thinks crazy things but won't say them out loud. It's all crystal clear. I'm pretty old now, and I can, with some accuracy, tell when someone's going to say something racist and to what degree. Now, can I do this with Lacey's razor-sharp ability? No. I'm not that skilled. But years of living in Omaha certainly add up to a pretty good spidey sense. I can certainly tell when someone's the scary type of racist. So a quick assessment of the people who work on the show tells me I don't have any of those guys around.

On the walls of the hallway right behind the studio, there is a picture of each person who works here on a clipboard, and each clipboard is drilled into the wall. So the hallway is covered in clipboards. At the bottom corner of the clipboards is a trash can. My picture is right above the trash can.

So one day I get called to the green room in the middle of the day. I figure it's a manager or agent or friend visiting, but I get to the room and it's a lady I have never seen before. She's a woman of color, so I should know her. She must not work anywhere near this floor. She is our HR lady. We work at a comedy show, but this woman is dead serious. She tells me there's been an incident. She says there was a length of rope in a knot hanging from my picture. It was reported by a coworker. She thinks someone hung a noose on my picture. I immediately laugh out loud. I laugh out loud in this woman's face at the *thought* of such a thing happening here. Not that it's impossible. It never is, but once she told me that, I knew exactly what had happened.

Almost everything in the studio is rigged with these little black ropes. These ropes temporarily hold a lot of things in place when there's a special set, or when giant set pieces have to fly in and out of the studio quickly. These pieces of rope are everywhere. It is clear to me that someone went to throw one of them away and it got caught on the screw that holds my clipboard in the wall. I ask to see the rope, and it in no way looks like a noose.

This woman makes sure that I know that there will be no repercussions for anything I say. She lets me know exactly what would happen to the person if we found them. She asks a million questions. "Has anyone ever said anything suspicious to you at work? Has anyone ever been mean to you at work? Have you ever gotten into it with anybody at work? Has anyone ever been inappropriate at work?" She gives me a million opportunities to take a long, hard look at how I am treated at work, and it leads me to one conclusion: I am spoiled to a hilarious degree.

She follows up with a phone call later in the week to make sure that I'm sure that I'm sure. I couldn't believe it. She did such a good job. I've certainly been at places where I would've killed to have someone like her around. It is so crazy that this woman is the opposite of Lacey's HR woman. The thought of someone being racist had this lady ready to go off! I loved her. I felt so well taken care of.

Let me tell you a story that is equally believable for me. Amber is kidnapped by aliens and they teach her how to sew. She wins *Project Runway* and becomes a fashion designer.

So, you would call my story unbelievable?

Yes.

IT'S A BIRD, IT'S A PLANE,
IT'S A REASON TO CALL THE COPS!

In order to bring attention to strong Black comic book characters and have a safe place to celebrate all things Black and nerdy, a group of Black nerds invented AfroComicCon. It was like a Comic-Con for Black nerds. They saw the success of O Comic Con (Omaha's version of Comic-Con) and thought, *What if we had something like that where Black people felt centered and welcome?*

So here's how O Comic Con went. Thousands of people wore whatever the hell they wanted. Full costumes with guns, knives, axes, swords, shields, and crazy prosthetics. Music was blasting, there was a ton of great food and really fun people. It was a three-day event. Lacey and her friends went and had a blast. Even though people were running around with, in many cases, real swords, they never noticed security or police officers. They felt welcome. They even had an after party! Everyone thoroughly enjoyed themselves. If their AfroCon was half of this, it would be worth it.

Encouraged, they choose a venue in North Omaha to host it. The venue agrees and they're one step closer. They have a meeting to solidify everything. In the meeting, the AfroCon team hands out what will be the poster. It outlines all of the acts and attractions. They begin their presentation and pitch what AfroCon would be. Outdoor music, cosplay. People dressing up as comic book characters. Food and music. Vendors and talks—stage combat class, comic book art class, making cardboard shields. I even hosted a talk with Black creatives! Extremely nerdy stuff. This is a small, somehow even nerdier version of O Comic Con. The venue loves it. It's all going to be pretty straightforward. They can do exactly what they want at the agreed-upon price (which is great because it's the first year of the event and they do not have a ton of money). The venue sees the value in this event for the community and can't wait to put this on! That is, until the police and the building's security start asking questions. Did I forget to tell you they were there? They were. The building's security sees one small detail:

"This DJ. He plays *R & B* music?"

"Yes. He does." They all examine the poster a little more closely.

"So this is *Afro*Con. Like Comic-Con but..."

"Centered around Black people. Yes."

This whole thing came unraveled because one of the acts was R & B. An eagle-eyed security guard saw this and pulled the thread. These idiots didn't realize that the "afro" in AfroCon meant Black people. The rules started to flow in. They could have their event but they would pay through the nose and it would be under a strict, watchful eye. Here's the list of rules they gave:

No outside music at all
No outside events at all
AfroCon would have to pay for extra security
AfroCon would have to pay for extra police officers (I'm not going to go into how cities all across America do this to keep Black events to a minimum, but I kinda just did.)
If you brought a plastic weapon, toy gun, or sword, it had to be sheathed at all times. If it wasn't, the many extra police officers and security guards would find you, zip tie

it to your sheath, and if you didn't have a sheath, they
would confiscate it.
No waving your weapons around
No actual axes or swords

The security guards and police estimated 5,000 people would come to this event. For Black nerds. In Omaha. There is no way that was ever going to be the case. But the more people they say will come, the more police and security we need, the more we will have to pay, so they overestimate. (Another tactic used by cities to keep Black events to a minimum, a thing which I will not go into.)

AfroCon finds the money and it's on. Lacey and I get there early to hang up signs that tell people where to park, where the entrances are, etc. We get out of the car and there are a ton of police there. A ton. It's me, Lacey, and a ton of police. The day goes on and the event gets going. It's almost all families and young nerds. The police force dwindles throughout the day. They see that it is just a big ol' bunch of nerds. We have wonderful indoor music, delicious food, and a great time.

No one was:

Shot
Killed
Stabbed
The victim of a drive-by

There was, however, Lacey's dancing, which she shoulda gone to jail for—holds finger to ear—aaaand, I'm hearing that it is I who is in fact the worse dancer. That is true. Neither of us great; me worse than Lacey.

I say all this to say, North Omaha has a bad rep.

We had a frigging blast at AfroCon. As a Black nerd, I really needed it. AfroCon took place right after news had just broken that there will be a live-action *Little Mermaid* with a Black girl playing Ariel. So Lacey is dressed as Ariel from *The Little Mermaid*. And one little girl, who had to be about six, came up to Lacey and said, "Who are you supposed to be?" Lacey replied, "The Little Mermaid." The kid looked at Lacey like she was crazy. "You can't be the Little Mermaid; the Little Mermaid is white!" Lacey explained to the little girl that that's what this whole thing is about. You can be whatever you wanna be. The little girl said, "Fine, but you're still not the Little Mermaid."

Her mother overheard this, grabbed her, and gave her a talking-to. The girl returned to Lacey with her mom close behind, the mother with arms crossed and giving her child the stink eye.

The little girl says, "My mom says we can all be whatever we want to be...And that I need to hang out with you more." Lacey and the mom laugh.

After AfroCon, Lacey goes back to her job at the opposite of AfroCon. She explained the event to her coworkers. Most were confused. A few thought it was interesting. Most didn't get it. A coworker asked, "How did it go?" Lacey explained that it was wonderful. She went over the many booths and performances and costumes. They were still talking once the morning meeting started. Lacey ends up telling everyone that she dressed as the Little Mermaid. "It was wonderful. My costume was amazing!"

The one true asshole at work asked, "*Who* did you dress up as?"

"The Little Mermaid."

He laughed and said, "You can't be the Little Mermaid! The Little Mermaid isn't Black!"

Lacey explained to him how the little Black girl told him the same thing. She talked to him about the fact that even she learned it's okay. He looked at her like she was talking crazy and said, "You aren't on that Colin Kaepernick shit, are you?" Can you imagine someone at your job saying this out loud and still having a job? Lacey is—and this goes without saying—the only Black person there.

Lacey told him to google why Colin Kaepernick is important. "I'm not gonna waste everyone's time. I also don't wanna go to jail." She spent the day retelling the story to many white people at work. No one knew why he was wrong to say that.

THE FIRST WORST JOB

A nineteen-year-old Lacey thinks she has a great job opportunity working at an online bill-paying service. On her first day, she is told she'd have to meet with the owner. "You're gonna love him. He always has a one-on-one with people on their first day. Don't be nervous. He's a big ol' teddy bear." When the time comes, Lacey is called into his office. She walks in and sits across from him in a regular office chair like the one he is sitting in. She looks at him. This man doesn't seem like a "big ol' teddy bear" at all. He says to her, "No, no don't sit there. Come sit here." He has a footstool next to his desk. He wants Lacey to sit on a footstool next to him so that he can intimidate her. This would not be the last time someone did this to her.

He says, "Are you Irish?"

"No."

"'Cause we have a lot of Irish people that work here."

Then he asks, "Are you Irish Catholic?"

"No."

"'Cause we have a lot of Irish Catholics that work here. Do you know what that means?"

Lacey knows damn well what that means. It means everyone's white but her. She doesn't answer. This book isn't long enough to get into why he did this the way he did and what that did for his ego.

He continues, "That means people act and behave a certain way. Do you think you can get along with those people?"

"Yes."

Lacey thinks this is the end of it, but he continues. "There's no stealing in my company. There's no horseplay of any kind. I need you to be a team player. I don't wanna hear any negative reports. I need you to fit in. Can you fit in?"

"Yes."

Lacey went back to her desk and cried. She quit the job the next day.

And if you're wondering about the difference between this job and the other more racist jobs, the difference is this: Lacey. It's always the individual person and wherever they are in their lives at that time. Sometimes it's easy to keep a job in a very racist environment, and sometimes all you need is one creep to make the place unbearable. There are worse stories than this and better ones. The reaction always varies because you can only put up with what you can put up with when you can put up with it. And here's a little reminder that we shouldn't have to put up with this shit AT ALL! But anyway, back to giggling about it.

Is This a Joke?

No! This is not a joke—unlike the state of race relations in America!

I don't want to scare you, but as you read these stories I want you to try to remember that Lacey and I are grown women who ended up okay. Okay?

So, shit is gonna get worse in this chapter. This is the chapter where I think it's going to become clearer just how frequent this stuff is. We are also going to take a look at a few racist bosses! Fun!

Y'all, we aren't even halfway through this book! And so far, we have really only been talking about stories that are okay to share with everyone. Wait. Isn't that insane? The very real fact that your stories of racism that have happened to you fit into little categories like this? It's true, they do! There's, like, "okay to talk about at work" racism and, like, "okay to talk about with your white friend racism," and "okay to talk about at home racism." These are three very different levels of story. Now, it's not healthy and god bless you if these aren't unspoken rules that you recognize. You live a different life than I do, a better life—and I am truly jealous.

I mean, anyone can say anything they want to anyone at all. It's just, personally, if I do the math of what will happen once I talk to a white person about the time a racist thing happened to me, it will not have been worth it. Now, the possibility always exists that they will be empathetic and understanding, but other reactions are possible, too. Sometimes you tell a person and they listen and then ask you why you didn't stand up for yourself. Or your having talked to them about this means they can ask you every question about race that pops into their mind forever. Or you see the weird way they not only can't relate but don't want to. And then you have to know that about them. It's hard to put into words, but it's a minefield I choose not to walk in. So, quick quiz for white people:

Question 1: Do I wanna talk about this stuff with you? Do most Black people?

Answer: No. Because it's a very big thing for us and a very little thing for you.

Question 2: When you talk to us about this stuff, do we get to see exactly where you fall on the racism spectrum?

Answer: Yes, and that shit cannot be unseen.

Question 3: Am I saying, "White people, don't talk to Black people about race"?

Answer: No. I'm saying, "No one wants to relive their traumatic events with someone who may say it was all their fault." You know?

Question 4: Am I saying, "Unless I'm at some event for this book or I know you extremely well, I, Amber Ruffin, do not want to talk to white people about racist things that have happened to me"? And would I even go so far as to say, "I don't want to have discussions about race with white people"?

Answer: I don't think every Black person feels that way. But—and I can't stress this enough—I very do.

You know, once, when I was very young (younger than I am now, if that's even possible!), I was on my way to an improv class. Literally as I arrived—my hand was on the door—I saw a very drunk man headed toward me. He was stumbling down the street and yelling at everything he saw. He saw me and gave me a scary look and called me a string of racial slurs. I quickly turned away from him and pulled the door open and jumped inside, slamming the door shut, and when I turned around I was literally face-to-face with my improv teacher. He was right there saying, "Howdy, Amber! How are you today?" I replied, "Today, sir, I am magnificent."

I say all that to say, we are trying to ease you into some harder-to-believe stories. Like these.

BEING BLACK AT THE DOCTOR'S OFFICE: TRY NOT TO BE

"Your bad attitude can't affect my good day!"
—Lacey Lamar

Lacey once had to get a checkup for her new job. She was going to be working closely with old folks and needed an "all clear" before she got started. So just in case she wanted to, she could open-mouth kiss all the old people.

Amber, I swear to god.

But she didn't open-mouth kiss anyone at work.

Thank you.

She tried to, but there were no takers.

Lacey has pinched me, so I will act right. So, Lacey goes into this new building she's never been in to see this doctor she has never seen before. Lacey wasn't entirely sure where exactly to go, but she found the suite number and walked in. Lacey goes up to the counter and sees a woman who is less than polite. Look, everyone has good days and bad days. So what, chicken butt. So Lacey happily greeted her and gave her name and a slip of paper that had her appointment information on it.

The lady was shocked that Lacey dared to give her a slip of paper. She angrily barked:

"The office *you* need is next door."

Dang! Lacey thought to herself. *Why did she hit the "you" so hard?* No matter. She went next door, and this office was packed. She took a number and sat down. Lacey waited for over an hour before she realized that that lady had taken one look at her and sent her to the WIC office! (WIC is the program that supplies food, child care, and health help to low-income parents. AKA food stamps.)

Lacey returned to the first office prepared to hurt everyone's feelings. She was ready to give a full Suzanne Sugarbaker[1] speech.

"Hello. You may remember me from earlier. I'm the woman you profiled. Even though I had a doctor's appointment here, you sent me next door to the WIC office without so much as letting me say a single thing. You were wrong—we all know that now. But before I go back there for my appointment with your *boss*, what was it about me that made you think I came to this building to go to the WIC office?" At this point all the woman's coworkers have gathered. They are shocked, or at least pretending to be. A few are enjoying it. "What is it about my face, hair, clothes, or demeanor that made it unnecessary to ask me why I was here? Do I look that healthy? You know what? Not to be a you, but I'd rather not take the time to listen to your reply. Can you tell the doctor his eleven-thirty is here and is late and that's your fault?"

> "Your bad attitude can't affect my good day!
> But if you somehow manage to turn my good
> day into a bad bay, I'm taking you with me."
> —Lacey Lamar

---

1   I have no business making a *Designing Women* reference. But if you got it, I need you to tweet at me and say, "Fear not, Amber. I, too, am old."

Speaking of profiling, it's not very often that Lacey has time to go to the doctor. But a few years ago, she felt she had to go because she was unbearably tired. Now, you might not know this, but Lacey needs only five hours of sleep a day. She's a machine. So if she is feeling tired, something is probably wrong. Worried, she goes to the doctor. She's had the same doctor that she has loved for years, a DOC (doctor of color), but every once in a while, she'd go to the office and end up having to see the other guy, an OWD (old white doctor).

A month and a half before she went to the doctor, she'd started taking iron supplements. She has always been a little anemic and assumed that was at least one of the problems, even though no one had told her. But her self-medicating wasn't doing anything. So she's at the doctor's office, talking to DOC, and she is listing her iron supplements and explaining to him that she's never been this exhausted. The DOC says, "Before we take any blood, let's take a look at your history."

As he's looking through her history, scrolling through her file, he is reading entries made by himself and OWD. Lacey says, "The last time I was here, they did some blood work." DOC says, "Oh! Your iron was dangerously low three months ago. I'm sure that's the problem." Lacey gasps. No one had told her this. No one had called her. No one had emailed her. No one had told her to eat more steak. Nothing. She lets him know and says, "You know, Black women have a lot of problems with being helped at the doctor. We're often misdiagnosed or not diagnosed at all. He should've prescribed something." Unable to bad-mouth his partner, DOC apologizes and says, "I understand exactly what you're saying. Several times people have come here for help, but when they got here and saw me face-to-face, they asked my race and then asked for a different doctor." The two of them spend a little bit of time talking about all the many times they have to professionally eat shit. It's nice. So then he goes, "We are gonna run some tests. You're doing the right thing with your supplements. Sometimes it takes two to three months for the supplements to make a difference. Three months ago your iron was low; let's see if it's higher today." As they wait, DOC continues to look through Lacey's medical history. He's reading off things in her history. Not like a checklist but sort of mumbling to himself like, "C-section, physical in December..." Stuff like that. As he's reading this list he just so happens to mumble, "...kidney stones..." and Lacey goes, "Did you say kidney stones? I've never had kidney stones." He looks at her and is like, "I'm afraid you did." They look at each other and just bust out laughing. "Five years ago you had a kidney stone. Did you go to the hospital?" Lacey remembers. "Oh my god. I did."

It was the middle of the night and she was having the worst stomach pains. Having given birth to a child before, she honestly believed that it was superstrong labor pains. Have you ever seen that show *I Didn't Know I Was Pregnant*? It's the frigging best. These women find out they're pregnant as a baby is coming out of them. There are enough of these stories to make an entire TV show. And let me tell you, it's good television. Anyway, Lacey went to the emergency room. She fills out the forms and they ask her if she is constipated. Lacey says no. "Are you constipated?" No. "Do you have diverticulitis? If you have it and eat popcorn, this can happen." She doesn't have that and doesn't like popcorn. She's in agony. They put her on pain meds. It's still pretty horrible. After the meds, she pees into that thing they have in the hospital bathroom that catches your pee. It's bad but she feels a little better. The meds must've really started to work. She goes home. Her prescription? Poop. They prescribed her to poop. That's it. That was their help. She never heard from them again. They must've gathered her pee and found out she'd passed a kidney stone, put "kidney stones" in her file, and never told her.

How does someone pass a kidney stone and not find out until five years later? Lacey told her white coworkers about this (her mistake if you ask me, but okay). This one idiot said, "Lacey, the same thing happened to me. I had extreme pain like you. Then, to my surprise, I was told by doctors I had a kidney stone."

Lacey: "When did you find out?"

Idiot: "The next day."

Lacey: "I found out five years later. It is not the same."

There are a few doctor stories, but we will just leave you with this one. When Lacey was pregnant, she had to do her own prenatal care. As it was getting closer to the birth, she went to the doctor, who said, "You should give birth any day now." But Lacey was worried. She would try to tell doctors and nurses that she didn't think the baby had dropped. As nice as they were, these doctors and nurses were uninterested. The doctor brushed her off, gave her the all clear, and left. She finally convinces a nurse that her concerns are valid. That the baby is damn near in her chest and giving birth would be near impossible. The nurse agrees. They get the ultrasound guy to come in. He does the ultrasound. Soon after, the doctor comes back in and says, "We are gonna have to do a C-section. Hey! If this had happened in the 1800s, you'd both be dead!" Y'all. What if Lacey hadn't convinced someone to give her an ultrasound?

IT'S HOT IN AFRICA

Working at smaller companies is good and bad. It's good because even if everyone is terrible, it's still fewer terrible people than in a very large company. Also, with a smaller workforce, you can change the tide a little more easily. You don't have to explain why something is racist forty different times to forty different frowning faces. You do it once, everyone's there, and they decide to listen or they don't. But sometimes joining a smaller company is not a good thing, because there is one monster of a person who works there and he has everyone right where he wants them.

Lacey worked as one of the directors at a small nursing home. It was fine and most of the people seemed normal. Bonus: most of the kitchen staff were Black, so there was someone to roll your eyes with when things got insane, and things did go insane in an unbelievable way. Things here would get so insane that Lacey would think, *I gotta start writing this shit down. No one's gonna believe me.* Okay, so one white man was in charge of the completely Black kitchen staff. Let's call him Biff.

Can I just quickly say that Amber was screaming laughing during this story. I had to turn my phone's volume down. She laughed so hard at my pain.

It's one of my favorites. My laughter was correct.

Okay, one day the staff complains to Lacey about the heat in the kitchen, which is odd because Lacey is not in charge of what's happening in the kitchen. But it is clear what's going on here; they are not being listened to by the white people who lead their department. They complained to Lacey because they thought she might listen to them. They said that the kitchen was too hot to begin with, but now it had become unbearable because the air conditioner had broken. They were scared that because of the new crazy temperatures someone was going to either faint or die. Sounds like something you gotta listen to people about, but okay. Also, this was a small retirement home but they could definitely afford to fix the air conditioner. They could afford to buy two air conditioners, throw one in the trash, and use the other one in the kitchen. So at the next meeting, Lacey brings this up. Biff thinks it's hilarious. He waves off their concerns.

"You know how I know they're making this up? Because they're all from Africa. It's not hot to them. They're used to it being a hundred degrees. They're from Africa. It's a hundred degrees there. It's hot in Africa."

This fool said, "It's hot in Africa." Now, we can be sure of a few things.

1. We are dealing with a big old dum-dee-dum-dum.
2. If he's willing to say this in front of Lacey, then when she's not there this man certainly says some SHIT.

During this fool's tirade, Lacey googles "Johannesburg temperature" on her phone. It was sixty-five degrees. The second he gets done talking, she shows everyone. Lacey has to school them about how the continent of Africa has a million different temperatures and to stop saying ignorant shit like this. They get an air conditioner. Lacey reports back to the kitchen staff and tells them the whole thing. They all laugh about the statement

"It's hot in Africa." Lacey realizes she's going to have to do this man's job while doing her own.

Do you think this would happen with any other group of people? What if everyone was from Seattle? If the sprinkler system was on and it was constantly raining inside, would he let it go because "it's always raining in Seattle"? Would he? Call in your replies to the Dr. Frasier Crane Show.

At every meeting, this man says something gross about his Black staff. Every single meeting, a new crazy thing. Lacey doesn't find this surprising because if you're dumb enough to go on a whole tirade about how Black people are impervious to heat, you can't be that smart. Every time, Lacey explains why whatever he said was a crazy thing to say. It's tiring.

Eventually, the nursing staff complains to Lacey that Biff was making racist comments to them. They tell her that Biff has been calling the Black nurses "hood rats." Not just referring to them as a bunch of hood rats but addressing them like, "Yo, hood rat." As if the word *hood rat* is each of their names. It goes without saying that he's never done this in front of Lacey. Only in front of people who are Black and who work underneath him. These nurses told Lacey that they'd complained but they were never listened to. Lacey would talk to him about it.

She asks Biff if he has been calling the Black nurses hood rats. He doesn't deny it. He even tried to defend using the term *hood rat*. "When I say 'hood rat' I mean it in a nice way. You know, hood rat. Like a hustler, a good worker." Lacey googled the definition and read it out loud to him.

"'Hood rat. Noun. Someone who has sex with everyone in the "hood" or neighborhood; the term is linked to the culture of the American ghettos and to hip-hop culture. A hood rat is often a poor woman who engages in sexual activity like a prostitute, but without charge and without being coerced.'"

"Well, I didn't know that and that's not how I mean it. I think it's a fine thing to say."

It's not. So Lacey complained to Barbara, their HR person. Even though everyone had complained about this man, maybe it would be different coming from Lacey. It wasn't. They had no choice but to go over her head.

Lacey calls the head of HR for the whole company, Kimberly. She explains to Kimberly everything that has been going on. Kimberly is shocked, you guys. She cannot believe what has happened. Kimberly tells Lacey, "We're going to have to open an investigation." She does.

When an investigation starts on anyone at this and at most companies, they make the accused leave the building so the staff feels safe telling the truth about them. They tell them to get their stuff and leave and they will call you when the results come. And only then will they find out if and when they're coming back. The very next day Biff was back in the building complaining that someone on his staff called corporate on him. This was not allowed. He took a trip to everyone's office and gave them each an earful, and tried to intimidate everyone under him. He did this to let them know to keep quiet. But it was too late.

Their executive director was told to interview the staff one by one and send the individual reports of what happened to Kimberly. Lacey watches as one by one all the Black staff get interviewed and one by one they come out looking hopeful. Everyone was thrilled to finally get all this off of their chest.

In Lacey's meeting, she tells her executive director everything.

She remembers every last time Biff said something crazy and it felt great. She can't be sure, but it looks like the executive director is just nodding her head a lot and not writing down exactly what Lacey is saying. But Lacey is talking a mile a minute, so maybe she's just writing down the gist. Or just the word *racist* really big so it takes up the whole piece of paper.

When all of the statements are given, Lacey waits for a call from corporate. Once you file a complaint, they do an investigation and get back to you. But it has been a while and Lacey hasn't heard anything. Then she sees him. BIFF IS BACK! How was he allowed to come back to work with all those terrible things people said about him? Lacey immediately calls Kimberly. She is shocked when she hears what Kimberly has to say:

"We never called you because no one complained."

Lacey can't believe it. There is no way on earth no one complained. Even if everyone else was lying to Lacey for fun, you still have Lacey's testimony. Lacey tells her that that is impossible. Kimberly assures Lacey that sometimes people aren't willing to go on the record to file formal complaints about people. Lacey realizes that Kimberly thinks she got scared and changed her story. Lacey assures her that no one did. There's a long pause as Kimberly realizes what has happened.

"Lacey, can you tell me what you said in your interview?"

Kimberly is not allowed to read anyone's reports out loud to Lacey. But she can compare the notes from Lacey's interview to what Lacey tells her now on the phone.

Lacey tells her. She tells her all of it, and Kimberly doesn't say a word. There's a long, long pause and a sigh. Lacey says, "I can tell from your reaction that that's not what's on my statement." Kimberly says, "Your statement is two sentences. It just says, 'Biff said he wasn't sure about his workers.' And 'It's hot in Africa.'"

IT'S HOT IN AFRICA! Oh my god, I love this story. Lacey is livid. Their executive director did this. Kimberly tells her, "Please don't say anything. I'll take care of it." Two days later Kimberly flies in. She lets everyone know she is going to conduct her own interviews. She says, "If these interviews don't match up with what you claim the staff told you, we will have a problem." They interview everyone again. The executive director and Biff are fired.

That director is replaced. Her replacement is told everything. She hears about the whole fiasco by talking to the white people who work there. They are the only people she ever speaks to. I guess she didn't like it, because this brand-new replacement woman during her first week of employment has the guts to say out loud in a meeting, "If one more person says something to me about racism, I'm gonna slap the taste outta their mouth!" She is so tired of doing her job after a week that she has a meltdown. She has a meltdown about having to deal with race before saying one word to a single Black employee. Lacey did not stay at this job very much longer.

Although Biff was bad, he had nothing on another kitchen manager. Let's call him Sal. Everyone warned Lacey that Sal was a legit crazy person and was not to be fucked with. They told her that he was extremely mean. Mean to the point that people would go out of their way not to deal with him. "If you complain about him, he'll get so mad that it won't be worth it." Sal was the head chef. He cooked food and left. He interacted with almost no one. He was a terror, but people figured out how to work around it.

This was an independent-living home. It was an extremely expensive place to live. These people paid top dollar. They were rich. Three times a day they were served in a fancy restaurant by dressed-up waiters and waitresses. They expected everything to be perfect. And frankly, for what they paid, it should be. Lacey's job was to keep them happy. Unfortunately, Lacey had received numerous complaints about the food. Her coworkers begged her not to, but she would have to talk to Sal.

Lacey gathered herself and went into the kitchen. Sal was mid-prep; he seemed very busy. Crap. This was a bad time but it had to be now, otherwise Lacey might never work up the nerve to come in here again. Lacey asked him if he had a second as politely as she could. He didn't seem too annoyed. He wiped his hands on his towel and walked over to her. Lacey explained in the nicest of ways that the residents complained about his food. She stuck to the facts and made sure she used the kindest words possible. It's Lacey! She's tiny. She's fun and nice; she's cute. What's the worst that could happen?

He punched her.

Now, not like out-and-out punched her, but he punched her. You know how people punch you in the shoulder like, "Hey, man! How's it going?" Well, that was what he was trying to play it off as. She let him know he'd have to do better and he socked her in the arm and said, "No problem, bud." He punched her much harder than he should have. He did this to make sure Lacey knew it wasn't okay to talk to him like that. To make sure that Lacey fell in line like everyone else. The thing about Lacey is, she's literally a bodybuilder. It is one of her hobbies. I'd put a picture in here, but she won't let me. Oh my god, yes she will! Look!

And, frankly, she could whoop my ass even though I have a foot and twenty pounds on her. So Sal punches Lacey in her rock-hard arm, and as a reflex Lacey immediately punches him back, also in the arm, with everything she's got. Lacey can throw a punch. But even if she couldn't, she's got enough muscle to make it hurt without any real form behind it. After she rocks this idiot, luckily, she has the wherewithal to say, "Right back atcha." His face looked shocked. He couldn't believe it. She had rattled his teeth. Lacey sauntered away like a cool frigging dude.

She is not a cool dude. As soon as she's out of sight, she runs to HR. She is one thousand percent sure she's gonna get fired. She bursts in and is like, "Sal punched me in the arm and I punched him back!" If she's gonna get fired, she's gonna take Sal down with her. The HR lady is used to doing whatever she has to do not to have to deal with Sal. She's no fool. She doesn't want her ass beat. And this woman looks Lacey dead in the eye and says, "Well . . . did you *tell* him you didn't *want* to be punched?"

No one does anything and they both get to keep their jobs.

HAIR STUFF OR CAN I PUT MY WHOLE HAND IN YOUR HAIR—OOPS, I JUST DID

One lovely Christmas Eve, I was in a department store getting some last-minute gifts. I was rocking my very cute afro puff and really feeling myself. I'd already had some compliments as I walked through the store, so this was turning out to be a good trip. All of a sudden, as I turn down an aisle, it feels like someone is trying to pull my hair off. What I feel is fingers going into the afro puff and pulling. I think, *Is Amber filming this as a joke? Is it my daughter? Why is this happening?* I then realize exactly what it was. Someone ran their hands through my hair, their hand got stuck, and they kept pulling to try to get it out. They struggled, and it's because they didn't know not to put your hand in an afro. You can't do that; you can't run anything through my hair. Not your hand, not a comb, nothing. If anything gets put in my hair or Amber's, for that matter, it belongs to the hair now.

I feel the hand leave my hair, I turn around, and a tiny white woman is standing there. The woman happily exclaims, "Oh my god, it's so fluffy. I just needed to feel it." What she didn't think would happen is that she would get her fingers tangled in it. This is why I don't like to wear the puff—it can get messed up too easily. Amber always tries to get me to do it so we can be twins, and sometimes I do. But I will say, there are too many curious white fingers in Omaha. This lady doesn't apologize at all. I look around and a lot of people have seen what has happened and are watching to see how this whole thing is gonna unfold. Little white lady just keeps talking. "Your hair is so pretty. I love it! You know, you people—" I cut her off right there. With as much kindness as I can muster, I say, "We don't touch people's hair. You don't touch my hair without permission and I don't touch yours without permission. Understand?" The lady nods and leaves. Nothing good ever comes after "you people." I had no choice but to cut her off. As I walk away, I see Black people are frozen in place all around me. I say to them, "I'm just trying not to go to jail today." They laugh and reply, "I wondered what you were gonna do."

I also have a buncha good hair stories. Not good hair as in "our society considers my hair good"—because hahaha THAT'S NOT THE CASE!—but good hair stories like stories about hair that are good. Okay, so when I was eighteen, it was time for me to get my first job. I wanted to work at a sandwich place with my friend. The sandwich place was in West Omaha, a part of town famous for its whiteness. Mom and Dad warned me that I should get a job on our side of town and that "if something happens and you need help, no one will be there. You'll look around and realize that you did this to yourself." I was like, "Okay, 1957, everything's going to be fine." Besides, I had my friend (a white girl) working there with me. That's when they gave me the best advice I've ever received: "You love your little white friends and they love you, but they have no idea what racism is or how to stand against it. If given the chance, they will leave you high and dry. Not because they hate you, but because they can't see what's happening."

Okay, so how dare they talk about my little white friend like that? But I'm eighteen. I have NO EARTHLY CLUE the type of rampant racism that lies ahead in life. My parents knew I was about to find out what real racism is. They tried to save me, but it had to happen.

Side story: I never went to college—too busy trying to have a career in sandwich making. But our sister Angie, who is now a reverend, went to an evangelical college and they were so racist that she couldn't stand it. She dropped out. The same thing happened to my niece. She got a scholarship to a very fancy rich kids' school and they were too racist, so she dropped out. (Don't worry, she still has a thousand more scholarships; she'll be fine.) Finding out what true racism is when you're eighteen seems to be the rule. Not, like, silly racism, but the racism the white people who are only ever around white people have.

Okay. So I'm at the sandwich place. It's fine. There's one horrible boss, Fran, and one less horrible boss, LHB. Every time Fran balances my drawer, I'm short; every time LHB does, I'm fine. Curious. The thing about Fran is she is the type of racist who sees what you have and is jealous. I had a sweet, cute kind boyfriend and I'd leave every night to hang out with her other employee, my little friend, without ever inviting her, and I have natural zazz. This hoe[1] could not stand it.

So, one day, my friend and I are cleaning up at the end of the night when Fran frigging unloads on me. She says a lot about who I date and how I look and it ends with:

"Your braids are so gross. Why won't you take them out and straighten your hair like the rest of you people do?"

I'm shocked. The whole thing was so venomous. It was like bullying but with racist stuff. We knew Fran was a dumpy bully, but racist? That was new. But none of that mattered. I was not alone! My little white friend would back me up, right? I'll never forget. I looked behind me to my friend for support and she was just standing there nodding her head. Agreeing with Fran! It hurt my little feelings so bad, y'all. She was my best bud. My parents were right. As time went on, every single one of my little white friends went on to say some insane shit. Not constantly and not a lot by any means, but stuff that would not fly today. Anyway, I was fired the next day. But I am so glad I learned that lesson as a kid. Can you imagine learning that at age thirty?

And I know this book is about Lacey, but one other short story first: A few years ago I was at my friend's office party and it was too much fun. Look, I always have a good time at office parties. Any party, really. I'm programmed for fun. I'm having fun right now, sitting in my kitchen, typing away about horrible stories that keep my family oppressed. So I'm at the bar ordering (I assume) a

---

1   Do you spell it ho or hoe? I've seen both and I prefer adding the extra "e." It just feels more fun. But I bet the most fun way to spell it is "heaux." I'm gonna try that one day.

margarita when the drunkest girl in the world walks up to me. She's a tiny drunk white woman who no one had ever heard speak. This woman is so drunk you can't understand what she's saying. Later, I would see Drunky outside waiting for a cab. She was being held up by another woman from the office while Drunky tried to kiss her and Office Woman was dodging her kisses while holding her up. Later, people reported the two of them standing next to a pile of puke. So that's the type of drunk this woman was.

But back to about an hour or so before that. Drunky comes up to me and talks to me about how much she loves my afro. And I will say it did look especially juicy that day. But before I could move away, Drunky put her whole hand into my fro. The whole hand! Not like touched it or bounced it or patted it, but did a magic trick where she "made her whole hand disappear"! I start to tell this lady not to put whole hands in people's hair lest she only be able to count to five for the rest of her life when— she loses her balance! Now again, we are at the bar and she tries to hold on to my hair for support, but it's not enough. With her whole hand in my hair, she does the only thing that would stop her from falling: She HOLDS ON TO MY HAIR FOR DEAR LIFE! AND IT HOLDS HER UP! Do you remember the poster for the movie *Cliffhanger*? Where Sylvester Stallone is facing certain death, dangling hundreds of feet in the air, holding on with just one hand to the edge of a cliff? Well, it's the same thing except my hair is the cliff and Drunky is Stallone. I've never been prouder of my hair. It literally saved someone. She is so drunk she doesn't know what she's done. I grab her so she doesn't fall. I prop her up against the bar and proceed to laugh myself sick. It was truly the funniest thing that could ever happen to an afro. Better than the time a dragonfly was trapped in it while I was in line at McDonald's and I cried until a stranger got it out. Better than when I used to do this bit where I'd hide a pencil in my afro and take it out during meetings. I still laugh when I think about that tiny woman being saved by my strong fro. My hair is a superhero.

Oh, no! This is the best afro story: Okay, so when I first moved to LA my friend wrote on a sketch show and he would put me in sketches. It was the coolest thing I had ever done! You get a cool trailer and people would come in and put makeup on you and ask what you want to wear! So at the time I had a TWA (teeny-weeny afro, and I don't know if you're supposed to repeat that. Probably best not to). I walk into the hair trailer and the lady is having a bad time. She tries to cover it up, but I can see it on her face. I sit down in her chair and am determined to make her feel better. I get her giggling a little bit and can see she's starting to calm down. She then looks at my TWA and asks me what wig I'm going to wear. I tell her I'm not going to wear one. I think to myself, *How rude that this lady just assumes I'm going to cover up my hair! Gross Eurocentric standards of beauty.* I assume that's gonna be the end of it, and I am so wrong. This woman freaks out. She's so flustered. She turns bright red and is like, "What? You're going to wear your hair like *this*? Like, how? How do you plan on…You mean just like *this*? Okay. Well, I don't know how to…What do you usually…How? HOW?"

And then, hand to god, she starts crying. Crying. I couldn't believe it. She looked at my afro and cried. My afro made her cry. You guys. While she sat there and did nothing, I put on a headband and called it good. I was no longer interested in her feelings. I left the trailer. It was not the last time I would have to do my own hair while sitting in the chair of a "professional."

Okay. Next story. Back to Lacey. Once, when Lacey was young, a thousand years ago,

I'll pinch you.

Please don't. Years ago, it was nighttime and Lacey was taking the city bus and when she got on it, the white lady bus driver looked at her like she was disgusted. She was giving her a full scowl. Now, if you're a bus driver in Omaha, Nebraska, I don't know your journey or what you have to go through. So you might just give everyone that look for your personal safety, and I respect that. Sometimes I do that. Lacey taught me: "If the sun is down, wear a frown." And I gotta say it has always worked for me. So Lacey gets scowled at by this lady and thinks nothing of it until the lady goes, "Geez! You look like you cut your hair with an ax! You look just like Gladys Knight!" She did not mean it as a compliment. This raggedy, bus-driving Gargamel was trying to burn her, but she ended up giving her a great compliment. Gladys Knight is as talented as she is beautiful, so shut your "Midnight Bus to North Omaha" behind up.

You'll never believe this one. AS WE WERE TALKING ABOUT THIS STORY, a complete stranger came up to me and told me I looked exactly like Gladys Knight. Did he have that thought independently? Did he hear us talking about it? I don't know. Do I look anything like Gladys Knight? No.

There is this thing where white women like to be loudly grossed out by the way Black women look. Our hair and bodies and stuff. And you can always see clean through it. Like, even though they're not saying it, what they're thinking seems to be, This *lady gets laid? Men like* this? It's like they're actively comparing themselves to you and their coming up short is infuriating. So they try to rag on you. It never quite works.

Pictures of Lacey's Different Hairstyles and What They've Been Called

Afro—"Cornrows"

Curly wig—"Real hair"

Straight wig—"Natural"

Natural—"Weave"

Dreadlocks — "Medusa Hair," "Worms," "Muslim Hair Covering,"
"These Things," "Hair Hat"

Once, when I had braids, they were called "locs" by a very woke white lady who cautioned us that we aren't saying "dreads" anymore because that term came from Christopher Columbus calling people's hair "dreadful locs." Now we just call 'em "locs." To keep ourselves moving forward. Please stop trying to educate me on my hair.

HISTORY LESSONS

As we have learned, sometimes something racist happens to you and you don't do a thing. You let people drown to death in a pool of racist thoughts and actions, as is your god-given right. You are only one person. You are not the Black ambassador to the United States. If people haven't figured it out, it's their problem. And sometimes you stand up and explain why they shouldn't be doing or saying whatever insane thing they said. Here are a few little stories where, for whatever reason, Lacey decided to help.

Lacey loves to tell stories about our family. There are five kids, and some pretty hilarious things have happened to us over the years. Ooh! Maybe the next book will be the fun stuff! Like when Jimmy got his head stuck in the crib bars or when Jimmy got stuck in the clothes chute! He's probably climbing through someone's HVAC right now. Anyway, Lacey was in a meeting talking about her life as she grew up with so many kids in the house. One of the directors chimed in and said it must have been hard on your mom being a single parent with five kids. Nowhere in the conversation did Lacey say that she was raised by a single mom, 'cause she was not. She told the director that she was raised by both our parents and that they are still married. There should have been an apology from this idiot where she said, "I'm sorry I'm such an idiot. I've been this way forever and I don't know how to stop it." Or, at the very least, that lady should have stopped speaking. Instead, she chimed in and said, "I mean usually you guys are raised by just your moms." Lacey gave them a history lesson explaining why that's a racist thing to say.

They hired a new supervisor at the retirement home Lacey worked at and you could tell he was not pleased when he met his current staff. He came to the directors' meeting complaining that "there needs to be more white staff working." That's enough right there, but this man, in front of other human beings, said, "I've looked at the staff we have and some are from Africa and I don't think they can even read. Can most people from Africa read? I mean, having more white people will just make this an easier work environment." Lacey explained how that's inaccurate, let them know the statistics for African immigrants and their grades, and why that's a racist thing to say. All of which was NEWS TO HIM. Lacey immediately reported him to HR and he was fired shortly thereafter.

While working at an Alzheimer's home, you become used to some residents using slurs. Lacey happened to befriend a new eighty-seven-year-old resident and she was very pleasant when they first met. And during Thanksgiving time, her family was visiting her in her room. Lacey walked in to greet them, a room full of the resident's children and her grandchildren. Her face lit up and she said, "Oh! Everyone, I want you to meet this n*****r girl!" Lacey was waiting for her family to correct her—families always do. They usually apologize with great embarrassment, like, "Oh my god, Mom! You can't say that!" They end up apologizing profusely. But this time not one person in this room seemed shocked or embarrassed. They all came around her and said, "It's great to meet you; my mom loves you." Lacey immediately gave a small history lesson on how we don't use the n-word anymore. And the old lady never used the n-word around Lacey ever again. Guess which of those sentences is a lie.

When working in management in Nebraska, it's not uncommon to be the only person of color. That's because people think "diversity" means hiring Black people in the lowest positions in their companies, thereby making sure to keep the system that makes it hard for Black people to succeed at that company in place. But that's not what this book is about. This book is about a doofus named Lacey.

Amber, you are hard to like.

Lacey was at a directors' meeting and everyone was acting really strange whenever they mentioned the new coworker starting that day. Lacey immediately knew she must be a person of color because they all kept asking her if she had seen her yet. She had not. They were dying to tell her but didn't know the right way to do it. During the meeting, one of the directors could not take it anymore. Finally, she blurted out, "There will be another colored gal working here now, Lacey!" She was so excited to tell her that she could not hold it in. Lacey had to give a history lesson on how we don't use the word *colored* anymore.

My new coworker and I had one thing in common: we were Black. Once she started, the staff and the residents at the retirement home could not tell us apart. Every day, people would mistake us for each other. I'm not in any way exaggerating. I'm a good fifteen years older than her.

She's fifteen years older than me, too.

Shut up. I have natural long locs and she has bone-straight shorter hair. I was in a meeting with my boss for thirty-two minutes—*thirty-two minutes*. When the meeting was over, she said to me, "Now send Lacey in because I'm supposed to meet with her soon." I said, "I am Lacey!" and we sat there in silence and then she apologized. I gave a lesson on how not being able to tell Black people apart is racist.

Everyone at Lacey's work had to agree on where their annual outing was gonna be. Paintball? Olive Garden? Who knows! Everyone voted unanimously to go to the shooting range, except for one holdout. Lacey. Lacey explained how, historically, that's gonna hafta be a big fat nope.

After Lacey had complained about many racist coworkers, one job required Lacey's whole office to go to diversity training. Lacey was the only one who showed up. I wish Lacey had the phone numbers of everyone in the world, because nothing is funnier than the texts she sent on this, the angriest day of her life. The next day, she explained to her coworkers why that was wrong.

Once, as a lady was inviting the staff to her dinner party, she says to Lacey, "Hey, Lacey, I'm having a dinner party. Gin and juice, right? Right? We have some for you! Gin and juice!" Now, this lady is very fun and nice. But she's as dumb as racism is real. Here's another thing she said that we will laugh about 'til we die. In order to understand it, you have to know that Lacey, who is straight, and was married, drove a small car. She comes up to Lacey and says, "You should date Emily! You guys would make a cute couple! 'Cause you both have those tiny lesbian cars—you know, the ones that lesbians drive? You know how they drive those cars in that area? You know, there's that one area that's full of lesbians and their tiny cars?" Now, lesbians have many stereo-types to choose from, but tiny cars ain't one of 'em. Subarus are not tiny. And I feel confident in saying that there is *no* place where lesbians meet up to drive tiny cars. How could anyone have come to that conclusion? In this instance, *we* learned this history lesson.

Lacey once worked at an office where almost all the super-visors were white and everyone else was Black. Their boss wanted to congratulate them on doing a good job so she bought a T-shirt for all the staff who did such a good job that says, "#wewinnin." The T-shirt was shown in the morning meeting. Lacey asked, "Why does it say 'we winnin'?" A coworker leaned over to her and said, "Because that's how you guys would say it." Lacey sent me this text as I was pitching this book:

> Hello!!!!! One more thing to add!! Our new shirts came today for reaching our goal. I asked why does it say that and I was told "because that's how you guys would say it."

Lacey explained how this is racist.

When the person who got those shirts left, Lacey was filled with hope. Until she met the replacement. He was a bit of a mess—let's call him Mess. Mess was never a huge problem, but he was definitely one of those people where you didn't know what in the world he was going to say next. Like, you could be pretty sure he wasn't gonna say anything intentionally hurtful, but you also knew that on any day he could say something that would make you have to file a report.

So, they work in North Omaha. Again, North Omaha is a large part of Omaha. With good and not-great neighborhoods. This particular part of Omaha is a very nice part. It's the same neighborhood my rich friend lives in. That's where we're at.

It's time for the morning meeting. There are plenty of Black employees there. Mess stands up to give an inspirational speech. "I want to make this building the jewel of Omaha. Now, I know it sounds crazy because we are in North Omaha, but I believe that even in this neighborhood we can make this building look great." He goes on, but you get it. All the Black people hear this and are giving each other the *Can you believe this guy?* eye. This fool is so stupid he doesn't realize what he has said. Lacey's the only Black director. She's gonna have to get up and say something.

"The Black people who work here are in an unfortunate spot because most of our directors are from small towns. We have to tolerate them talking about how they're scared to come to work and how they're scared to walk to their car—even while the sun is up—as if someone wants to steal a 2003 Kia. North Omaha is everything north of Dodge! Warren Buffett damn near lives in North Omaha. If he is fine here, I think you'll be fine here. Please stop acting like North Omaha is a bad place to be.

We grew up here. Stop talking about the place we grew up in, live in, and love with disgust."

This was the same place where, on her first day, Lacey looks around and the employees are dressed like you wouldn't believe. The woman showing her the ropes was dressed like she was getting ready to paint a house. Throughout the office she sees people in torn jeans, sweatshirts, T-shirts. From the directors down to the mail guy, everyone is dressed like they're about to put on a production of *Oliver!* Lacey asks why everyone is dressed like this. And would you believe that this lady fixes her face to say, "We dress this way because of the neighborhood we are in. It's very poor and very Black. These people aren't used to seeing people dressed up. When people see us dressed up, it intimidates them. We dress this way so that we can be on their level." She dresses down to be on Black people's level. If she had dressed as fancily as possible, she could not have been on our level. From where she is, she cannot see our "level" without a telescope. It was clear this woman had never heard of church.

BEST SUPERVISOR EVER!

Here's a story about the best supervisor Lacey has ever had. One day, Lacey came in to work talking about a new program that gives African children laptops. It's a new kind of laptop that can be manufactured for a hundred dollars a pop. A charity made and distributed as many as possible to connect African children to the Internet and give them a voice in the global dialogue. Lacey was talking about how great it was. As she was going on and on about progress and how these children can finally be heard and how interesting it will be to hear their stories, the best supervisor she's ever had could not stop laughing. Between his giggle fits, he said, "What are African kids gonna do with laptops? What are they gonna do with it? Okay, they'll learn things, but what will they do with what they learn?" It ended with him saying, "Well, I don't see the point and I'm against it." To not understand it is one terrible thing, but to be against it is a second kind of terrible! How can you be against children learning? Two terribles for the price of one? In this economy?

Of all the supervisors Lacey has had in her life, that man said the fewest racist things. The man who said the fewest racist things out loud had the deepest, most stank racist belief just festering in his heart. "I'm against it." It's the quiet ones, y'all.

And, for contrast, here's a story about one of my bosses!

A million years ago, I used to work at a comedy theater. Throughout my career, I've worked at a few. I landed this job as an actor/writer/improviser at this place after having a full-time job writing and performing comedy for, like, five years. I wasn't green, but none of the jobs I had had were in this city, so to a lot of people I seemed to come out of nowhere. It was the best learning experience and I made some real friends for life while I was there. There was a bar across the street we would drink at almost every night. At that bar, there was a Black bouncer who would always be there, ready to talk shit and give out hugs. He would always tell me how proud he was of me. It was a magical time. Now, when you work at a regular job and someone says something racist to you, you have to do all kinds of special maneuvers, but if you're a comedian, you can just say, "Say something like that again and see if I don't break your leg." Everyone laughs, the idiot gets the point, and you can save face. Only the two of you know you are dead serious. It's great. And, because most comedy shows want only one Black person, you make the rules for how Black people are treated. No one's ever going to go, "Well, Marcus lets me call *him* darkie. He says it's funny." That's the trade-off you make. It may be lonely, but you don't have to put up with anything like that for the most part.

So we do this show at this theater and it goes really well, so well that the city's big-deal newspaper does an article on it. It's gonna be a huge piece in the Sunday edition. We go downtown to the office and take pictures at a studio! Fancy! There are six people in the cast. The person writing the article divides us into two groups to talk to us. We think nothing of it at the time, but the two groups they put us in are:

Group 1: three white people
Group 2: me, the gay guy, and the Hispanic guy

I can't remember the questions they ask us, but none of them stick out as crazy or suspect at the time. We end the interview and get back to work and forget all about it.

A Sunday or two later, I wake up with a million voice mails on my phone. I immediately assume someone has died. I listen to the first voice mail. It's a guy who works at the theater. I don't know him very well, but his message is something like, "Hey, man, I'm sorry about the article in the Sunday paper. That's messed up and if you want me to say something, I will." Fuck.

What in the world does the article say? I get up, get dressed, and walk to the corner store as I listen to the rest of the voice mails. They all say the same thing. I snatch up the paper and head back to my apartment. I find our article! It's cool! There's a million pictures of us. The cast looks happy and cute and in love 'cause we are! I read the article and I get to the part everyone's talking about. It's a quote from one of my castmates that says:

"When you're straight and white in the improv community, it takes ten years to get cast in a show. I think Amber's been here for twelve whole minutes."

People were livid. And they had a right to be. Look, even right now I'm a million years old, I've been doing comedy professionally full-time for more than fifteen years, and people *still* want to act like I don't know what I'm doing. I think it makes them feel better about where they are in life if I only ever got anything because I'm Black. Their own mediocrity never crosses their mind.

Frankly, the fact that that guy said that did not shock me or hurt my feelings. At this point, I had known him for a while. I knew who he was and didn't really care. The fact that he felt that way didn't bother me in the slightest. At this point, I had been out in the world away from Omaha for quite some time, making my own way in various comedy theaters. He was not the first to say that and would not be the last!

> "I could do what you do on *Late Night with Seth Meyers*, I just choose not to."
> —A thirty-year-old white male improviser
> who could never

So I thought, *Well, that sucks, but it's not that bad. It's just one guy.* Then I read the rest of the article. The whole article was about diversity. They had segregated us to talk to us about diversity. What a shitty theater for allowing them to do that to us, what a shitty paper for allowing one of their people to do that to us, and mostly what a horrible conniving person that turd of a reporter must be. I hope they find this and understand the fact that they are a bad human being. Before I was done reading the article, I would read a quote from the owner of the theater that would send me into a white-hot state of rage forever:

"I know some casts over the years have not been happy about the emphasis on diversity. There's a feeling that the most talented improviser should get the job, period. But it's also about content. It's also about being truthful to the community you live in. Someone who isn't the best improviser may have a lot to say."

This sent me into a white-hot rage. Look, that one guy saying that one idiotic thing that negates my talent is fine. People know him. They know he's liable to say anything. Also, his feeling like that was a secret only to white people. I would've had money on him saying that out loud to my face by then. Hey, whatever it takes to make yourself feel better. But the *owner* of the theater in an article about whether or not he should have hired the only two minorities in the goddamn show? This insinuates that we aren't talented! This is also something people love to do. They love to act like there were no Black people good enough. No one wants to be like, "Hmmm. I've never met a Black person I thought was actually good enough to be in my little show. Maybe I'm a piece-of-shit racist who can't relate to anything a Black person says, judges them before they've said it, and thinks Black people are funny only as stereotypes, but when they're stereotypes, I look down on them." Honestly, I know this sounds crazy, but there are people who think, *Black people just aren't good at this*. About, like, a ton of stuff. But COMEDY? We literally use it to survive. I'm doing it RIGHT NOW.

Anyway, my boss had shown his whole ass and would need to pay.

I call Mom, Lacey, and Angie and ask them how to handle this butthole of a situation. I don't want to, but I'm going to have to talk to this guy. That day I get two important phone calls that make me feel a lot better. One is from the lady who was in this cast before I replaced her. I made the decision to take this job, in part, based on the fact that they actually told me I would be in the cast *with* her. But when I got there, it turned out I had replaced her. She called me and encouraged me and talked to me about the kind of place it was and their blind spots and what they had done to her. She gave me a lot of talking points. She really helped me out.

The other call was from our director, who was almost as mad as I was. He assured me that the owner of the theater who said all those things in the paper wasn't even in the room when I was hired. The director also had never heard of that owner being a part of casting a show—ever. He had no hand in the casting whatsoever. He told me, "I cast you because you're great. You got the job because you were the best person for the job." This really made me feel a lot better. I reach back in my mind and conjure up this conversation whenever I've let someone get to me.

Now there's nothing left to do but go have a talk with the owner. I have my talking points and I'm going to be calm and get through to him. I know it's not my job, but a lot of Black kids are about to come after me and I need to do what I can while I have some leverage to make sure they're treated right. I would do this for the children. Like Ol' Dirty Bastard once said: "Wu-Tang is for the children. We teach the children."

I go into his office for our meeting. My heart is beating a mile a minute. I'm nervous and ashamed and mad. He starts by immediately apologizing for what he said. I feel myself start to calm down. He goes on about the history of the theater and all their outreach programs. Outreach programs? Does this man think I'm here to pat him on the back for his work with the Black community? He must see my eyebrows change shape because he starts talking about how last year he was in a really bad place, and how hard his life was a year ago and how he's struggling to keep it together. He's trying to get me to pity him. What the fuck does that have to do with what we are talking about? That fucking tears it. I do not need to hear why this man needs my sympathy. And how dare he make this about him and his feelings? All this fool had to say was "I'm a crazy poop and I'll try to not be." But he tried to get me to feel SORRY for him, and in that moment, all the talking points my mom and my sisters told me slipped my mind and I fucking lost it. Y'all. I went insane. I start yelling and go on for a while. I'm screaming. Among the many insane things I yell at my *boss* are "Do you know how many people think that this theater only hires minorities to fill a quota? From now on, as long as this theater exists, they can have that thought, look to the owner of the theater for affirmation, and you're dumb enough to have given it to them! You're creating a bunch of white men who feel threatened by my mere existence!" (We didn't have the word *incels* then.)

Anyway, say what you want about this man, but he let me cuss him up one side and down the other. He apologized again, and even though I cussed out my boss, I kept my job. I live in the exact opposite world as Lacey.

Ooh! Side story. Once, another Black actress at that theater was asked out to lunch by the owner and he started the lunch by saying, "So! How's your family in Omaha?" She said, that's Amber Ruffin. Not me. She excused herself, went to the bathroom and cried, sucked it up, came back, and was a delight to be around. The two of them had a fun lunch. Now, did he think she was me? Who's to say? But he definitely did.

I Do Not Care for These Stories

I wouldn't believe these stories either, but hey, they happened. In this chapter, things are about to get gross, y'all. We're gonna take a look at some stories that still have me saying, "What the fuck?" Most of these have special surprise endings. I mean, they *would be* surprising if you read them anywhere other than in this book.

We were taught how to handle unfair situations by our mother. She was very Mrs. Huxtable about everything. She always calmly presented idiots with proof that they were being idiots and let them trap themselves. It's masterful. She's a very smart lady. She's an extremely intelligent and extremely cool dude. There are countless times when I watched her handle a teacher or furniture salesman who was being racist or sexist like a boss. It was the best way to learn. And, unfortunately, a necessary thing growing up in Omaha. I've seen her handle a million situations with grace, but there were three times in my whole life when I remember her really sticking it to someone. Now, you would think if you spend years and years of your life taking care of your kids, sacrificing, being the perfect mommy, they would, bare minimum, not write a book that has the three times you were less than cordial to someone who deserved to be punched in the mouth, but here we are. That's why this section is called:

MY MOTHER, THE EXECUTIONER

One afternoon, the day before Thanksgiving, I was working on my homework in the living room when the doorbell rang. At this time, our neighborhood was maybe 50/50 Black/white. There was little to no crime, my elementary school was great, and there was no reason for me not to open the door. I looked out the window and saw a white woman and her daughter. The woman was forty-something and her child was a teenager. They were dressed like they had just come from church. I opened the door. When you're a kid, there's nothing better than opening the door to a stranger. *What do they want? Why are they here? Is it Dad's coworker? Did we order a pizza?* It could only be fun. Now, these people were all smiles and so was I. I was a kid and the world was good. There's no way someone would ever show up to your house to deliver racism! The woman had a big box of food. A turkey, canned goods, dessert stuff, treats. It was a huge box of goodies! I looked at the box and was so excited at the thought of free food. The woman said something like, "This is for you! We at [whatever church she was from] are doing our best to make sure every family has a great Thanksgiving!" I took the box from her and I exclaimed, "You're just *giving* us all this food for free?"

What I didn't understand was that sometimes churches go to poor neighborhoods and give out Thanksgiving care packages. This woman and her child came to our neighborhood and thought they were in the ghetto. OUR NEIGHBOR HAS A POOL WITH A SLIDE. These people are too lazy to go where their gift might actually be needed. Omaha has real project housing, people who may really need this food, and they decide to come to our neighborhood 'cause it has some Black people in it. And some is more than the none they're used to.

My mother heard me shout to some white lady about "giving us food" and knew instantly what was up. She tore down the hallway, snatched the giant box from me, and told me to go to my room. As I did, I remember hearing her say with a level of disgust I'd never heard before, "You brought your *child* with you?" My mom continued to enlighten this woman, but she was speaking in hushed tones so I wouldn't know how bad the world is yet, and she was likely destroying this little white girl's faith in her mom.

It wasn't until years later that I understood what had happened. This poor idiot and her kid were pretending to do good and, worst of all, wasting all that food.

When I was in maybe third grade I was really into arts and crafts. I tried a little bit of everything. I loved looking in our children's encyclopedias for different crafts you can do and the countries they come from and other boring PBS crap. I liked learning about different arts and crafts and what they were called so I could use the word *macrame*. It never came in handy; I'm pretty sure this is the first time I ever used that word. I would sit in my room for hours with old magazines, cut them up and put the tiny pieces in separate piles sorted by color, slather a piece of cardboard with glue, and make mosaics. It was truly the most fun, and, writing this, I realize crafts are what my life's been missing.

Googles "scrapbooking," realizes it's just too much, decides life's full enough.

So I came home with this library book and I was enthralled. It was some old arts and crafts book from, I think, the sixties? I sit on the couch and get to planning my next adventure! As I'm reading this book, I come across something I've never seen before. Something called a golliwog. A doll with a black face and big red lips, hair in five poofy, short ponytails, and raggedy clothes. I immediately hate the fact that there is a craft that I am not familiar with. I'm a third-grade craft expert! How could this happen? And it is presented in a way that's like, "Everyone knows what this is and here's *our* version of it." So I wonder if this is a real thing or if these people just made it up. There's only one person to ask: Mommy! I walk up to her and give her the book and ask her about this doll. She is immediately infuriated. This woman picks up the phone to call our elementary school. A little insight into who Mom is—the school's phone number is memorized. Simultaneously, she opens the book, looks at the copyright date, and asks for the librarian. Bit of backstory: my mother has helped out a lot around the school and I'm the youngest of five, so these people know my mom by now. Perpetual Room Mother, Cafeteria Cashier, Head Baker for All Bake Sales, Teacher's Assistant, PTA President, Safe House before and after school. They have to know something bad's about to happen. So Mom gets the librarian on the phone and calmly rips her a new one for exposing her child to racist imagery. She tells this librarian exactly what golliwogs are and where they come from and what it means to Black people. Y'all, if I could've written down what she said to this librarian, I would've gotten an A in African American studies. Before she hangs up, she explains what danger this seemingly harmless book puts Black and white children in. She takes the book and explains to me that we live in a house full of books and there are a lot to choose from. I would need to read one of those. This ancient arts and crafts book is no longer an option.

My stories about Mom verbally executing people are like these artful, well-thought-out, beautiful speeches she made that have just the right amount of meanness and spunk. I learned so much from watching her shake people out of their ignorance with her words. But, once, things went a little differently.

I have heard what is known in the Ruffin family as "The Tale of Disneyland's Parking Lot." It goes as follows: We five children were in the van with Mom, excited and ready for a fun day at Disneyland, when Mom pulled in to a parking spot that someone felt they had a right to. That person was very mad. So mad that he yelled, "Fuckin' n*****!" He yelled that to a woman in a van full of children! Mom, without missing a beat, flips this dude the bird and replies, "I got your n***** right here, bitch." And this little bitch proved his supreme bitchtitude because he drove away silent, scared of a five-foot-one-inch 120-pound woman. She then turned to Lacey and Angie, the only ones who heard, and said, "Don't tell your father I did that."

Which brings us to an unexpected part of this book called "Your Options."

YOUR OPTIONS

When you are in a racist situation, you have many options. It always depends on what situation you're in, what they've said, who's with you, and how far you are from home. Your safety comes first. So sometimes it seems as though you're making a crazy decision but what you're really doing is staying safe. Here are some of your options:

You can do nothing.
Doing nothing is always fun. You just let whatever racist thing that happened happen. The person looks you dead in the eye after having said some nutzo stuff and, unbothered, you return their gaze, forcing them to think you haven't been listening. If done right, it can be pretty fun.

You can walk away.
This one is one of my favorites. When someone says something crazy nowadays, I like to, midsentence, walk away and never return. You can also wait until they're done speaking and hold eye contact. They'll expect you to start talking but you never do! In fact, you leave!

You can calmly talk to the person and hope they'll see your side of things.
This is for religious people or young, good people who are full of life, laughter, and love. I don't do this one anymore, so Godspeed.

You can expose them as the dumbass they are.
This can simply be accomplished by telling the truth! I think

this is the most common thing to do. It's still fun and you don't have to feel like you acquiesced.

You can hurt their feelings.

They really crossed the line or you're drunk or you have just had it. And this is the risk people run when they say something racist— they don't know where they fall on the list of dumb racist stuff you've heard that day. They could be the first or the fortieth thing! And, because eating shit is bad for you, if it happens frequently enough, at some point you're just gonna snap on a racist. The good thing about it is, it's a moment they learn from and will likely never forget. And you are always completely justified.

You can invite them to make their words match their actions, or back the fuck off.

When people say the n-word, they're looking for something. You might feel like giving them what they're looking for! Now, this last option comes in handy more than you'd think. See, when you're a little, nicely put-together Black lady, a lot of people think you are to be messed with. They think they can bring their racism to you, so they can get the—high?—of being a big bad supremacist. They think you can be played, and if you shy away from them, they may just see how far they can push you. It's like handling a bully at school. Sometimes the way not to get your ass beat is to demand a person fight you. And when they realize they are too big a wimp to do that, they understand the world a little bit better. In some ways, it's more helpful than calmly talking to them!

My dad is gonna be so disappointed at the amount of foul language in this book! Side story: Here's who Dad is: He is, like, the happiest, nicest, most soft-spoken man in the world. Which, frankly, opens him up to a lot of being bothered for fun. Dad likes to take a nap when he gets home from work. He has sleep apnea and is no good without his nap. Whenever he sleeps during the day, I bother him for fun. He's too tired to get up, so you can't get in trouble. It's a great time. I like to knock on his door and serenade him with the same song every time. The hit song "Sleepy Daddy" to the tune of the most beautiful song in the world: "Reflection" from the Disney musical *Mulan*. It always goes like this:

(I knock on the door. Dad wakes up to say:)

DAD: Yes?

AMBER: ♫ Look at me. You may think you see that dad is awake.

But my daddy's sleepy. Every day, he sleeps at the same old time.

Now I see, if I wake him up, I can have some fun, but it's gonna make him maaaad. ♫

DAD: Amber, get out of here with that. I'm trying to sleep now.

(I leave. Five minutes later, I knock on the door.)

DAD: Yes?

AMBER: ♫ I am now in a world where I have to hide my song and how loud I sing it.

But somehow I will show my dad just how loud I sing until he tells me to stop. ♫

DAD: Why are you doing this? If you don't get out of here, you're gonna get it.

(I leave. Five minutes later, I knock on the door.)

DAD: Amber, you better not be—

AMBER: ♫ WHOOOOOO IS MY SLEEPY DAD? IS HE

DREAMING? IS HE MAD? WHY IS SLEEPY DADDY SOME-
ONE I DON'T KNOW? I WON'T PRETEND THAT I'M GONNA
STOP FOR BEDTIME. ♬

DAD: (Throws shoe) Get out! Get out! This isn't funny. I'm
trying to sleep!

AMBER: ♬ When will sleepy daddy show who ♬ Sing
it, Dad!

DAD: No. Get out of here.

AMBER: ♬ Who he is insiiiiide! ♬

Not my best parody but it's the only way I can get my dad to
sleep. And then, at the end, I take a bow and, I'm not kidding,
after all that, he APPLAUDS! He gives me a literal round of
applause because the song is over and he feels his child did a
good job. He can't help it! He's too nice! Anyway, in case you're
wondering, that's who Dad is.

Speaking of Mom and Dad, we aren't going to get into their
stories but I do think I have to tell this one. My parents were
both in the air force, and that's why our family lives in Omaha.
There's an air force base in Bellevue, right outside of Omaha,
that they had been stationed at and they just decided to stay
here. Our parents saw that North Omaha was underserved in
many ways, so they decided to start a day-care center.

They moved to North Omaha in the 1970s and bought an
elder-care center and converted it into a day-care center. In the
basement was a cafeteria, outside was a whole playground,
and the main floor was a giant playroom. It was a pretty cool
place full of books and toys.

Turns out, North Omaha had no other real day cares at that
time. So their place filled up fast. It got to the point where
almost every Black family in Omaha had a kid there. To this day,

people pull me aside and say, "Are you a Ruffin? Your mom and dad used to babysit me! Tell them my family says hello!" Then you come home and tell Mom and Dad that their family says hello and, without fail, they go, "Oh! I remember them! What a sweet child. Just a joy to have around." If a person exists who Mr. and Mrs. Ruffin don't like, you don't wanna meet 'em.

So the day care is going great. Mom and Dad are the first day care to offer flu shots in the Midwest, they figure out how to accept government assistance for child care so a lot of parents in the neighborhood can afford them; they really feel like they're a part of the community. They even get a day-care van to pick up and drop off children. In fact, before their day-care van, State Farm had no other such vans in the Midwest, so Mom, Dad, and State Farm had to sit down and invent their insurance policy. Neat, huh?

Anyway, Mom and Dad are making a lot of money at this day care and doing quite well. I mean, it's a lot of money. They renovated our house. It was *the* picture of seventies glamour: shag carpeting, woven wood curtains, and an orange fun-house-mirrored bar. I can't describe it; it was just so very cool. They have our oldest two sisters and things are looking up.

After years of success, they have two facilities, twenty-two staff members, and around 200 children. They are visited by the woman whose job it is to decide which facilities can receive money from the government. Jill Bratcher. She sees Mom and Dad and their success and is not pleased. During her visit, she looks at the books and, out loud, says, "How could you have cleared this much money? *You* cleared this much money?" She runs the numbers again and again, sure that they've got it wrong. Mom steps away for a second and comes back and Jill Bratcher is cussing out one of the teachers. Mom tells her that we don't talk to our staff like that. Jill Bratcher says, "Come on. You know you guys use profanity." This woman thinks it's okay to come into this place with Black people and start cussing at them. Because we are Black and Black people cuss a lot. Even in a frigging day-care center full of children! She's crazy. But Mom's standing up for her employee has made Jill Bratcher very upset.

Jill Bratcher works in an office next to one of Mom's good friends, Sheila. Later that same day, Sheila calls Mom and says she just heard the woman in the next office say, "Theresa Ruffin doesn't know who she's dealing with." Sheila and Mom have a talk about Jill Bratcher. Mom remembers her saying that Jill was "very punitive." She had never heard anyone use the word *punitive* about a person. Mom starts getting phone calls from kids' parents saying, "Someone visited my house and told me I have to pull my kids out of your day care." Now, ninety percent of the kids in the day care received government assistance. If the government took them off of the list of subsidized day cares, there wouldn't be enough kids to keep the day care open. But, more importantly, there would be a period of time where 200 children had nowhere to go to be taken care of while their parents worked.

There are different health inspectors assigned to different zones. And after Jill's visit, when it's time for the health inspector to come, everyone sees it's a brand-new guy. Not just any guy, the guy who is in charge of inspecting the boys' home way out in West Omaha. He was famous for giving them failing grades and *that* place has the support of millionaires. So Mom and Dad know what they're in for. This man is visibly grossed out to even have to be here. And even though they never have before, this time, they fail their test. But, like, not over little stuff. Over big stuff that would take some renovation to fix. Jill Bratcher immediately takes Mom and Dad's day care off the list and shuts them down. This woman takes away twenty-two jobs and leaves 200 kids without a place to go. She could not deal with Black people being this successful. My parents sell it, and it re-opens later with different owners and zero renovations.

Our parents had five perfect kids and great lives. They're fine. The two of them are probably giggling right now over a drawing one of their grandchildren made for them. But have you ever heard of such movie shit in your whole life? Every few years I remember that story and am blown to pieces.

I never tell white people that story because they can't frigging stand hearing it. Honestly, they look like they're in pain as they're listening to me tell it and are annoyed that they have to carry this information around with them. I have never been able to understand why white people have such a low tolerance for hearing about racism. I mean, we have to *live* it! The least you could do is nod your head. The previous and the following are just two of the many reasons why Black people don't want to talk about race with you.

One time I was talking about some racist something or other with a bunch of improvisers and this guy gets up from his chair and screams, I mean screams out of nowhere, "Irish people had it worse than Black people! We weren't given jobs and were arrested all the time! You don't hear *us* complaining about it!" A grown man shouted that at me not too long ago.

This grown man's friend is the guy who has a very specific kind of racist tic. Okay, so sometimes there's this thing where white people have lost an argument about a Black issue and you, just by being Black, become a place where they can relive that argument, and this time say all the things they didn't say before and win. They can win this argument and this time no one will call them racist or shortsighted. If you're Black and this doesn't sound familiar to you, consider the number of times your white friend has tried to get you to say you like the Beastie Boys. I mean, that alone is elevendy-million.

So this guy loves to calmly start conversations with me about Black stuff and gets mad when I don't say what he wants me to say. It's little but I see it. It's hilarious and I love it. He's never very mad; he's always just, like, visibly frustrated. It's all "Can you believe this celebrity said this racist thing?" type of stuff, always wanting me to be like, "It's okay to say racist things." And, of course, I never do. It's fun.

Another thing he does is, like, use me to kind of yell at all Black people. You know? He'll say things to me that he wishes he could yell to all Black people. Let me see if I can get you to understand it. One day he's talking to me about being a college student and he talks about how hard it was and I empathize and say something about how hard it is to not have a lot of money and be living on ramen and good times. He whips around to me and is instantly mad. He kind of yells at me but in a hushed tone so no one can hear it, "I didn't have a lot of money at all in college but I wasn't *poor*. I budgeted smart. Just because you don't have a lot of money doesn't mean you have to be poor. Poor people just don't know how to make a budget and stick with it." And I can't describe it to you, but the way he said that to me was just—you know, he was working through some stuff. People love to get mad at poor Black people when they eat out, go to Chuck E. Cheese, or drive a car. It's truly the gateway racist talking point. It comes right after "Black people just *love* me" and "Oh no! Black people have started moving into my neighborhood!" And he knows you can't "budget yourself" into upper-lower class. If you could, he wouldn't have said it quietly, so that only I could hear it. He would have said it in a normal voice. So this guy likes to get little jabs in here and there. He uses me to work through his racist thoughts and feelings. It's nuts.

Oh! I know what it's like! It's like when a guy is sexually harassing you and he'll whisper disgusting things to you so no one hears. And as soon as someone else walks in the room, he'll act normal as if he wasn't whispering to you about his gross weiner. It's a mess. Men are a mess.

I say all this to tell you that one day this guy is talking to me about I forget what, and he asks me for my honest opinion and I give it to him and it hurts his feelings. It hurts his feelings worse than I intended. Later that day, I end up talking about that story about my parents and the day-care center and later he pulls me aside and, in that same uber-frustrated whisper-yell, he goes, "That story about your parents? I think they were idiots to let that happen to them." He starts laughing and walks away.

See, Lacey? I know some comic book villains, too!

What are you even bragging about?

Yeah. I don't know.

HERE'S A LIST OF HEAD-SCRATCHERS

In the break room one day, Lacey's sitting with two white female coworkers. They're talking about how crazy their weekends were. One lady really winds it up like she's about to tell the scariest story in the world.

"I'm on this elevator, right? All by myself. And these two big Black men get on. The door closes and it's just me and these two big Black men."

She stops telling her story. Lacey goes, "Well? What happened?" The girl says, "That's it. That's the end of the story." Her big story was "I ONCE WAS OUTNUMBERED ON AN ELEVATOR." For all we know, she could've been in there with my dad and brother, her only danger overhearing a discussion about whether Magneto is the strongest supervillain.

Please just say he is. Do not get Dad started.

Another time, Lacey went to her gas station. The same one she always went to. No one was ever mean to her there. She had honestly never given these people an extra thought in her whole life. Just normal Omaha-nice, happy-seeming people. Now, I don't know if you remember this story, but this was the day after a Black man named Charles Ramsey helped rescue three white women who were being held captive in a house. It was all over the news. America was so happy to have found those women and so proud of Mr. Ramsey. When Lacey went inside to pay, the gas station attendant was unusually excited to see her. He said to her, "Did you hear the story about the man that rescued those girls yesterday? See, Black people can do good things, too!"

He said, "See?" as if *I* was the one who didn't think Black people could do good things even though I am one and some made me. Did he think I had low self-esteem and Charles Ramsey could give me the courage I need to believe in myself? What exactly was that? You know what, this book is gonna leave some people with more questions than answers.

But there really is only one answer:

Racism.

Racism.
    Council Bluffs MAD DADS.
    Everyone remembers MADD, Mothers Against Drunk Driving. Well, years ago, North Omaha had something called MAD DADS. It's our local chapter of an organization made up of dads who were so concerned that they took to the streets to make sure young kids in North Omaha were staying out of trouble. They were a group of Black, tough-talking dads whose television appearances made you feel happy. Like a big group of dad best friends who got together weekly to care about their community and show little Black kids that someone was there for them. I forget what that stands for exactly...aaaand a quick Google search has revealed their acronym: Men Against Destruction-Defending Against Drugs and Social-Disorder.
    Lacey was driving in Council Bluffs, Iowa, with her two little friends. Council Bluffs lies just over the river but is truly, in every other sense, miles away. Now, I know I'm from a place that makes people say, "They don't have Black people there,"

but in Council Bluffs, Iowa, they really don't have Black people there. So everyone loves to tell you how if you go into Council Bluffs, you have to be careful. It's 11:00 p.m. in the middle of winter. It is well below freezing. As these three Black teenage girls are driving home, the car shuts down and then rolls to a stop. Terrified, they try the car again. It goes forward a few feet and stops again. The engine won't even turn over at this point.

They're going to have to get out and walk. In no way are they dressed to do that. They check their surroundings. In front of them is nothing and no one. Behind them is nothing and, really far away, there's a van parked on the street. Next to them is an old building. To their right is a closed restaurant. There is no place to walk to to get help. There are no cell phones to use to call for help. It won't be long before the car becomes too cold to stand.

They get out and put the hood up—universal sign for distress, right? Their only hope is for a car to drive by and take pity on them. Maybe they could flag them down and the driver would stop and save them. Few things about this:

What are the odds someone is going to stop for three Black teenagers? SLIM.

Nothing says that a crazy person won't stop for them, pick them up, and eat them.

Dicey as it is, it's really the only option.

As they sit in the car, remembering their old lives, imagining their funerals where people will surely shake their heads and say, "That's what they get for going to Council Bluffs," they see a cop car in the rearview. They're excited, because surely this means they're saved! Few things about this:

That's how you know they were young. To be excited to be alone with the police with no witnesses is, and I say this with love, dumb.

They lay on the horn to try to get the attention of the police car. As the car drives by, it doesn't slow down one bit. Several more cars drive by and don't slow down either. I mean, it's a honking car on the side of the road. No one can blame them. This goes on for another two hours.

Things are looking grim. They look behind them and that van that they thought was empty, sitting a block away, is suddenly a lot closer than it used to be. There's also someone in it. All they can do is watch this future murderer become inspired. They keep an eye on him while honking at every car that goes by. Then the girls truly lose their minds when the van starts to move. As they watch this big, old, nondescript van slowly head their way, they are certain it will be what kills them. They look to the old restaurant parking lot and now there's a car there, also slowly headed for them. So this makes two cars when there were none. Now a third car is pulling up next to them. Before they know it, they are surrounded by three cars. They are gonna die. A man gets out of the van to—they assume—kill them. He stands next to his van for a while, just staring at them, before approaching their car. Goodbye, cruel world. He knocks on the window. Lacey yells, "We are not rolling down this window." He keeps knocking on the window and their conversation goes like this:

Scary: What are you doing here?

Idiot Children: What do you think we are doing here? The car doesn't work. It died.

Scary: You're lying! We saw your car move!

(Remember, they have been sitting here for hours, freezing in a car that is off. If this man saw this car move, he's been watching them for hours.)

Scary: Are you waiting for drugs? What are you doing here? We saw the car move!

Idiot Children: That was a long time ago. No one waits for drugs in the middle of nowhere for hours.

Scary proceeds to pull out a walkie-talkie and discuss the situation with the people in the other two cars. After a short, stupid discussion, he says:

Scary: We are with the Council Bluffs MAD DADS. We can get you guys some help; we can drive you to the gas station.

Nooooow, I'm not in charge of the MAD DADS, but I have never, and I mean never, seen a group of MAD DADS who were white. And I kind of feel like they were MAD DAD–ing wrong. The Omaha MAD DADS wanted to protect their community. But it seemed like the Council Bluffs MAD DADS wanted to catch some Black people. This man watched three teenagers almost freeze to death on the side of the road hoping that he could watch a drug deal go down, then god knows what he would have done. Seriously. What if our dad had come to save them and this old van-driving dumb-as-rocks walking turd saw it? He could have done anything. Anyway, Scary gives the "all clear" into the walkie-talkie. They look behind them to the van and A WIFE AND TWO KIDS POP UP. THIS MAN BROUGHT HIS FAMILY TO WHAT HE THOUGHT WAS A DRUG DEAL.

They were so excited at the thought of catching drug dealers that they let three teenagers freeze in a car for close to three hours.

LEARNING IS FUNDAMENTAL

Before Lacey started working at the girls' rehabilitation community, she had to take a psychiatric behavior training class. This would be a great opportunity to learn how to give the children what they needed and be able to understand them better. Lacey (big nerd) was excited to learn. Their instructor was a middle-aged white guy who couldn't hide his ignorance when talking to POC in class. He'd walk in and give a completely normal greeting to everyone, but when he was talking to minority students he'd be like, "Yo, yo, yo. You gotcho assignment?" Or "Yo, yo, you gon' be here 'morrow?" The second this started, Lacey wasn't having any of it. This isn't the most uncommon occurrence. She didn't let him act this way for one minute because it's truly the most annoying thing. Here are some examples:

What They Say to Your Class-mates	What They Say to You
Hello, everyone!	yo, Yo, YO!
Oopsie, you miscalculated.	Biiitch, you trippin'!
Correct!	You right, you right.
Give it a shot!	It's like you ain't even be tryin'!

What They Say to Your Class-mates	What They Say to You
Which way to the interstate?	How I'm posta get home?
We did a good job and hit our goal!	We winnin'!

Not only could Lacey not stand being talked to like this three times a week for the next eight weeks, but she noticed there were a lot of young Black kids just starting out in this class with her. They shouldn't have to deal with this fool. She told him he couldn't continue like this. "It's ignorant and offensive. I realize you're trying to be cool. It's not. Talk to us like you talk to everyone else." He did not like that at all. Oh, well. She wasn't there to make him feel comfy in his ignorance. She was paying money for this class. And anytime I'm paying you money, basic respect better be included.

It quickly became clear to Lacey that this man was in no way qualified to teach this class. He was a next-level dum-dum. He would teach them made-up facts. It got so bad Lacey would record him so we could all listen and laugh. My favorite thing this guy ever said and the straw that broke the camel's back was this:

He once was trying to explain the difference between the prefixes *supra-* and *super-*. Now, I don't know if you're about to google *supra-*, but this teacher didn't. He told a class full of adults a made-up definition of an actual word. Personally,

I would've leaned in, enthralled. But Lacey was livid. He then said the dumbest thing any human being has ever said. He told the class that *supra-* comes from the word *supracalifragilistic-expialidocious*. He said *supra-* means "above," and that's why Mary Poppins always held the umbrella "above" her head.

I mean there's like a million insane things in that line of thought, but I'm gonna just say this: Where else could you possibly hold an umbrella? Below? Also it's not SUPRA-califragilisticexpiali-docious It's SUPER-califragilisticexpialidocious. Now, this may sound like this man has some real problems, but it was more that he wanted to hear himself talk and thought he didn't need to follow along with the curriculum. All he had to do was read aloud from the book or tell them to and he would've been saved.

Side story: Lacey had a Black friend whose nickname was Odo but her whole name was Odomichi. The two of them were at a gallery opening. It was a fancy gathering full of fancy people. A woman introduces herself to the two of them and asks what Odo is short for. Odo replies, "Odomichi." The woman is floored. Not only is that an impossible name to say, but it is also insane! She is yelling about it, going on and on. Multiple attempts to say it correctly. She can't. It's as hilarious to her as it is impossible to say. "It's like a crazy African name!" She goes on and on. Lacey laughs along and goes, "Oh yeah! It's like...What's that song in that Mary Poppins movie? The one that's really hard to say?" The woman, without missing a beat, says, "Supercalifragilisticexpialidocious!" Lacey says, "That's right. Now, how in the world is that so easy to say but Odomichi, a four-syllable word, is not? Hmmm. It's almost like you *want* to get it wrong." The woman sees her mistake but it's too late. Silenced, she skulks away.

Back to the story. Lacey was furious that she spent money on listening to the ramblings of a crazy person when she could've been learning things that would help her in her job taking care of children. She, along with many other students, went to the office, told them about his excessive use of the word *Yo*, and complained about his making up his own facts. Lucky for her, she had recorded his *supra-* rant. She played it for the people in the office, and they couldn't believe their ears. They must've talked to him, because the next day in class he tried to get his revenge.

He announced that they were going to learn about different cultures and their behaviors. "First, we are going to learn AAALLLLLLLL about Black culture." He walks up to the TV in the front of the class. With a smirk, he puts on the movie *Boyz n the Hood*. Most of the class, including several white students, walk out. They go to the front office again and make their complaint. They can't believe he's showing a movie instead of following the curriculum. He is immediately fired.

But the real end of the story and the part that makes it one of the best stories of all time is: The three students who stayed in the room later told the rest of the class that in the middle of the movie, a porn film started playing. Not only was he disrespectful enough to show them *Boyz n the Hood* and talk about "This is how you learn about Black people," but he was disrespectful enough to use his tape of that movie, which everyone agrees is a masterpiece, to record porn. He ran up to the TV and shut it off as fast as he could and ended class early.

Let's Take a Break and Have Some More Silly Stories

N o. This is where we are at now and it will only become more unbelievable. It's time for some real doozies. You'd think the stories in this chapter were plot points in a bad movie. And they are! *Lacey and the Whites* is coming to theaters this fall!

COWORKER QUOTES: NOT THINGS I HEARD, THINGS WHITE PEOPLE SAID DIRECTLY TO LACEY'S BEAUTIFUL FACE

"Omaha has some really racist gangs."

In a meeting someone said, "A lot of the time when you take braids down, you'll find roaches in them." I was wearing braids in this meeting.

"Well, I was fired by a woman who didn't pay me enough and always hired—umm . . . a *certain* ethnic group." I'm the only Black person in the room.

"Inner-city kids shouldn't get fireworks! Their parents

should spend their money on paying their bills and feeding their kids."

"Lacey, I started watching a show on Netflix about a Black kid playing basketball on a scholarship. I'm just trying to learn about *you*." "Well, I'm five-two and high maintenance so I don't think it's me you're learning about."

"We had a Black coach at school. He had a bald, lumpy, black head so we called him Milk Dud and he didn't like it."

"I was gonna vote for Obama but then I found out he was gonna paint the White House purple, so I didn't."

"There has to be something in the Asian DNA to make them look and become so smart."

"Muslims burned down Notre Dame. It has to be."

"Oh! I didn't know your sister Amber wasn't gay. She just reads gay. I mean, I should know." This was said by the lady at work who has to tell you she's gay every half hour in the hopes that she can say inappropriate Black stuff, but that's not how it works.

"Just because I only have vanilla cupcakes doesn't mean I'm racist. Hey, I liked chocolate back in the day; I used to swing in the jungle." This was also said by the lady at work who has to tell you she's gay every half hour in the hopes that she can say inappropriate Black stuff, but that's not how it works.

"Make sure you vote tomorrow so we can keep Trump in office!"

"I'm Native American and it was the Mexicans who put Native Americans in concentration camps. Not white people." A confused white person.

"There's a horde of MS-13 gang members on their way here to kill us."

Me: My African dance troupe is performing this weekend. So come out if you want to have fun!

Anne Marie: Oh! I don't know if I would like that.

Me: Why not?

Anne Marie: Because don't you guys perform naked with tambourines?

SALLY, THE COWORKER WITH THE LOUDEST, DUMBEST BELIEFS

These are all stories about Lacey's coworker Sally. Now, Sally wasn't the most racist coworker, or the loudest coworker. But what she was was a perfect mix of the two that guaranteed daily unease. As you read these stories, please imagine, like, a "no-nonsense" mother of five with chunky highlights and lowlights in her *Long Island Medium* haircut. She's the type of woman who wears shorts when it is cold. She's the type of woman who will keep your conversation going no matter what room she has wandered off to. Not the kind of woman who will send her meal back at a restaurant, but the kind of woman who will have fun with your kid when you bring them in to the office. The type of woman who will announce loudly to the room when you come in in a new shirt. When music plays, she sings along at full volume. If you feel sad, you can talk to her and she will be eager to try to provide some comfort and bring you a cupcake later. I give this long description just as a reminder that very racist people aren't always easy to spot. So here are things that a lady who most people would describe as a "delight" said:

Lacey went to lunch with Sally and another white coworker.

As they're driving through the parking lot in a strip mall connected to a grocery store, Sally sees a Black woman pushing a cart of groceries. Just a regular woman pushing a cart of groceries to her car. Sally sees this and says, "Oh god, it must be the first of the month." That was her reaction to a Black woman trying to shop.

"We need to stop hiring Black people. The ones we have are just ghetto, ghetto, ghetto! Lacey, I'm not talking to you. I like ya!"

Sally could not stand the Amish, Mormons, or minorities.

"The Amish are destroying this country. They rape the land." This woman said the land is being raped. "They get land from the government that they don't deserve and then they rape it." What in the world could she mean by that? Does she mean they "start farms and work the land"? Does she think "work" means "rape"?

Sally's friend Kate would chime in on her racist comments and say, "The time is coming soon where we will just have to build a commune and I will be the first one to defend it. I'll be the one standing there with a rifle. I won't ask questions. If you step on my property, I WILL SHOOT." These two women were supervisors.

Think about being a nineteen-year-old Black CNA. You had to listen to comments like these all the time. You cannot make these comments and have a job in America. If you're reading this and you or someone you know makes comments like these at work or anywhere, please contact the Sally and Kate commune. They have a lot of room and no real plan. Read more about it at www.unpopularcommune.com.

THE NO-NOS

Here's a few unlikable stories. I call them the No-Nos because as Lacey was telling me each of these, I was holding my head in my hands, peeking through, saying, "No, no, no, no, no."

Asian Mom

Lacey is talking about this very book with a lady she met at a party. The lady has two Asian sons who are adopted. Lacey said, "I'm sure you deal with these kinds of ignorant comments all the time, because people say all kinds of things about Asians. In fact, do you know what a coworker of mine once had the nerve to say to me about Asians? She said, 'You can't tell 'em apart; there's no way to know if they're male or female.' Isn't that insane? How could someone ever come to that conclusion?" This woman's reply was unbelievable, so, to make it easier for you to digest, I've taken what she said sentence by sentence and marked each one with a corresponding number of racist-ness so that you can make sure to know how Lacey is feeling as her reply hits her ears. A 1 is "not racist" and a 10 is "very racist." Ready? Okay. This white mother of two Asian kids said:

"Well, actually, Asians *do* look alike." Now, what she's saying here is that the thing Lacey explained to her is racist, is in fact not. I'ma go ahead and call that a 10 right out the gate.

"Different ethnic groups look alike. Like Chinese and Japanese people look like one another, then Vietnamese and Thai people look just alike." Interesting move. So, at this point, she could have backpedaled and said, "I mean people who are from the same country look alike." But she didn't. She said the opposite of that. She basically said that not only do Asians look alike, here's proof that I've spent time thinking about it. I would call this also a 10.

"Sometimes it's hard to tell them apart with their slanty eyes." (You guessed it—she pulled back the corners of her eyes to demonstrate.) "It's even hard to tell if an Asian person is male or female because Asian men wear lots of pinks and pastels. And that's confusing for a lot of Americans." I know that last quote took some twists and turns, but each individual word of that sentence is a 45.

Normally, Lacey would walk away from such insanity, but this woman has Asian children she's saying god knows what to. When Lacey tries to explain that no one can look at a white person and go, "You're from Finland. I can see that," why do they expect to do the same with Asian people? What is that? If you can't tell whether someone's from Germany or Denmark, then maybe all white people look alike. Anyway, when Lacey tries to convince her that she's just spouted a series of ever-increasingly crazy things, this woman says, "Well, we'll just have to disagree." Some party.

STEM

Lacey's child's school had a meeting for teachers and parents of girls involved in STEM. They were talking about the importance of young girls being introduced to math. And, most importantly, *how* they're introduced to it. Lacey said she's always been bad at math and the speaker said, That's not true. Someone *told* you that. The Black woman leading the talk told the parents that women, Black women especially, have been told in school that they're bad at math. All the Black women there nod their heads and begin telling stories about how their teachers all came to the conclusion that they're bad at math. Lacey told this story:

In elementary school, Lacey always thought she was good at math. She always got great grades. She was constantly the teacher's pet and was eager to do a good job. Now, in elementary school, when you're supersmart, the only way you know it is your grades. There aren't any special classes or groups or anything. But on the first day of seventh grade, Lacey got to take honors math class. Finally! She would get to be in the smarty-pants class with smarty-pants children just like herself. She could be the true nerd she was always meant to be.

Lacey walked confidently into honors math class. Like in all classes, she sat in the front. The reason for this is three-fold. I used to do it, too. One, because we have poor eyesight, and two, so we don't get distracted by kids goofing off. And three, so teachers can see how perfect we are. The extreme nerd in her would have it no other way. In this class, she was the only Black girl. But that's not a scary thing yet. Not in the seventh grade. In ninth grade, you may realize the situation you're in, but in seventh grade, it's still all fun. So on this first day of honors math class, the teacher began by calling students up one by one to do problems on the board. Some got it right, some didn't. When they got it right the teacher gave a loud, satisfying "That is correct," and when they got it wrong he said, "That is incorrect," and then explained what exactly went wrong. He wasn't too mean about it. It was just a way to get rid of some common mistakes early on. Lacey wasn't scared because so far, she knew every answer to every problem. Even in this best-of-the-best nerd class! It was the validation she always craved!

When it was Lacey's turn, she went up to the board and easily solved her problem. She put the chalk down and went back to her seat. The teacher checked her work and instead of saying, "That is correct," he said, "Wait. Come back. I need you to solve *this* one." Lacey knew some shit was about to go down. He had done this to no one else and she knew something wasn't right. She also knew this man was not happy she solved it. She also knew why. Even in seventh grade you know why. But Lacey is only a seventh-grader. She is unbroken. After being praised in elementary school, she thought she was the shit. It was on.

He put an even harder problem on the board. One much more difficult than everyone else's had been to this point. She solved it. She waited for her "That is correct," but she got no such response. He heaved a heavy sigh. This man is clearly upset. A child doing a good job at what he has asked them to do has made this grown man mad. He then puts a math problem on the board the likes of which Lacey has never seen before. Lacey looks back to the class; not a single face seems to register "This is odd behavior." She looks back at this teacher's gross smirk. He won. Lacey just looked at him and said, "I don't know how to solve this." He said, "That's what I thought. Now take a seat in the back." Lacey moved her stuff to the back of the class. She never ever raised her hand in that class. The teacher never asked her another question, and she never offered any answers. Thus began her fear of math. She never took another honors math class again. Lacey even began skipping math class. But I'm not supposed to write that part in the book. So if you see her, pretend you don't know.

Once, while at parent-teacher conferences, Lacey told one

of her child's teachers that story and he cried. He cried real tears. He kept loudly repeating, "That's horrible!" And then—and this is not a joke—he showed her how smart she was by giving her a few math problems on the board. All of these questions were AP algebra questions. She solved them easily and wondered what could have been.

The speaker at the STEM talk said, "Never tell a Black woman she's bad at math." She then opened up the conversation, and this bunch of Black women were heard and encouraged. See? Good stuff happens, too. In fact, the next book is just gonna be all the times we were affirmed in our experiences as Black women. It'll be one short-ass book.

Cotton Gin

So by the time Lacey got to high school, she pretty much knew the score. She could see the world for what it was and even understood that she could use this time as a high school student to try to make a difference. Lacey went to a high school in downtown Omaha. It was probably twenty-five percent Black.

Lacey was a part of a group of kids who got together and asked if they could have a Black history class. They expected an instant no, but instead the school had fifty thousand meetings about it. Student council, school counselors, vice principal, principal, student rally meetings—all kinds of stuff. All to talk about why it would be beneficial. Y'all. They couldn't figure out why Black history class would be beneficial. They would have these meetings in the middle of the school day and before and after school. After one of the meetings in the middle of the school day, the kids returned to class. Lacey and three other

Black students return to their history class. They walk into Mr. Lanklin's class and everyone's silently reading. There were only a few minutes left of class, so it must have been free reading time. Mr. Lanklin sees them arrive, stands up, and says, "Turn your books to page 129." This is odd, that he just shot up like that, but okay. They do what he says. There's a small paragraph at the bottom of the page. He reads only the first sentence of it: "'Eli Whitney invented the cotton gin.' There. There's your Black history." He slammed the book down on his desk and sat back down.

Side note: Mr. Lanklin was a scary person. And so was his wife. She was a teacher at Lacey's elementary school. And although she never had her as a teacher herself, it was common knowledge that she was an actual witch with superpowers. I have no proof of this, but I also have no proof that this is not true. Word on the playground was that she was one of those witches that could cast spells and loved to torture children. Everyone knew that when you walked near Mrs. Lanklin, you had to cross your fingers or she would turn you into a frog.

President

In high school Lacey was helping Tasha, a Black girl, run for class president. Their group of friends were all sitting in the common area along with everyone else who was running for student government. There was an hour given to all candidates to make their posters during the school day. Tasha is the first Black girl at Central High School to run for president. Surrounded by white kids and their friends making posters, Tasha and her Black crew are feeling proud of her, sitting at the table hard at work. One of the counselors comes over.

"What are you doing here?"

"Making posters."

"This is only for kids who are serious about running for class president. I need you to leave. This isn't for kids who just want to miss class."

The girls are sitting there with a pile of posters, markers, and posterboard. They are *clearly* making posters. This counselor went on and on. It escalated. Tasha was the type of girl to run for class president. She wasn't about to take this lying down. The counselor got angry. He took the posterboard THEY BOUGHT, folded it in half, and threw it out.

Lacey, still a stone-cold do-good nerd, had never seen an adult act like this. It scared her. She left. She's not proud of leaving her friends there. But she did. That counselor was scary.

A white kid won.

It didn't take her long to figure out how the system worked. She began constantly protesting racism at her school. Twenty-five years later, a white woman walked up to her in the supermarket and said, "Weren't you the girl who wore the 'Racism Is an Illness, Are You Sick?' shirt at school all the time?" Yes, she was.

THE DRAMA OF MISS BELL

Lacey's always been into the arts. Painting, singing, acting. I think every Ruffin is pretty artsy. In high school, Lacey thought it was time to try being in plays and musicals. There was only one problem: the drama teacher was an awful human being.

Lacey's best friend in high school was Mario. Mario and Lacey loved drama class and musicals. They would rent musicals from Blockbuster and watch them. They would get together and watch PBS musical specials. It was Omaha, so they had to make do. The two of them noticed that every musical at their high school had no Black people in it. If you were Black, you had no hope of getting the lead role. It was just an understood fact. So, facts be damned, they decided to try out for the lead. Who knows! Maybe they would have a chance. The drama teacher did like the two of them, which was more than they could say for a lot of people. So they audition for the lead roles in the school play. They read the lead roles in their audition and nail it. Who knows what'll happen, but they feel great about the job they did. The next day, the results are posted. Lacey and Mario, even though they auditioned for the lead roles, were cast as the servants!

That was *not* what they'd auditioned for. They were disappointed. They approached Miss Bell and asked why they were cast as the servants. She proudly replied, "Because when you auditioned for them, you did such a great job!" Lacey said, "We didn't try out for those roles. Do you even remember what we read?" They called her out in front of everyone. After class she asked them to stay behind. "Don't you ever question my authority again. Don't you realize if you were to move to NYC right now, you would never get the main roles in a show? This is the best you will ever get. You should be glad I let you play the servants." At this point, Lacey and Mario are too old to take this lying down. They take the complaint to the principal. In their meeting are Lacey, Mario, the principal, a counselor, and Miss Bell. They're all sitting around a big table. Lacey and Mario repeat everything Miss Bell said to them. The principal and counselor find this unbelievable. You can see it on their faces. "I know Miss Bell, and she is too sweet a soul to say anything like this." Before they can say anything to that effect, Miss Bell starts crying. "Why would you say that? How can you pretend I would do something so terrible?" Without missing a beat, Lacey applauds her and says, "Bravo. I guess that is why you're the drama teacher." It was her word against theirs. Lacey and Mario were never cast in a play or musical.

A quick note about white tears: Why? Why do they work so well? It's truly a great defense against being called a racist. I mean, it doesn't work for Black people. Can you imagine if Black people cried every time we were called a name? Every time we were accused of something we didn't do? Tell you what, I would be carrying around tissues at all times (not just when I go see musicals). I think, when a white person accused of racism cries, people think, *Oh no. I need to fix this. White people shouldn't cry. They should never have to cry!* I think when white people see white people cry, they relate and feel sorry for them. And when white people see Black people cry, they can't relate. Even though Black people have a billion things to cry about. Maybe it just boils down to the fact that white vulnerability is valuable and Black vulnerability puts the Black person in danger.

I did not expect this book to get this deep, y'all. Dang. We are ending up in unexpected places all over this book! ***raises margarita*** To the journey!

FUN STORIES ABOUT KIDS!

Dana

Lacey's best friend from kindergarten through the fifth grade was Dana. A very nice little white girl who lived down the street. When they were five, Lacey and her other best friend, Laura, a little Black girl, found Dana sitting on the swings all alone and they immediately became the Three Musketeers. They had a whole elementary school career together until one day, in the fifth grade, as Lacey was leaving their house, Dana's mom said, "I think it's time Dana spends more time with friends that look like her." The three of them never hung out together again. I wonder if Dana was sad or if she was like, "Good. I've been needing some new friends."

The Summer Arts Program

When Lacey was in the fourth grade, she got to go to the gifted summer arts program. It was this really cool summer course where kids who were extra-talented artists would go learn things about art that they didn't have the time or resources to teach you in elementary school. It took place in this big, beautiful classroom with tables instead of desks. It had three teachers instead of one, so everyone got a ton of special attention. The geek in Lacey was so excited. She arrived with a backpack full of special art supplies Mom bought for her. She arrived early, chose a spot at a table in the front of the class. All of the children laid out their supplies. Each kid had brought different supplies, but everyone had crayons. And that's where Lacey had 'em beat. Lacey didn't have any ordinary crayons; she had a big, brand-new box of Chubbies crayons! Chubbies had just come out and no one had them yet. By having them, Lacey was truly stuntin' on these hoes. As we were writing this I told Lacey I didn't remember what Chubbies crayons were and she got mad.

If you had to google it, too, tweet at me, "Amber, it's okay that you didn't remember it." And if you did remember what Chubbies crayons were, tweet at Lacey, "Lacey, it's okay Amber didn't remember it." But do google it, because they are cute.

Lacey perfectly organizes everything on her table. She takes great care to set the Chubbies out in the upper-left-hand corner. A perfect place. Before class starts, one of the teachers, let's call her Crayon Karen, walks around and greets every child. But when she got to Lacey, instead of greeting her, saying hello, or making sure she felt welcome, Crayon Karen came over and snatched Lacey's Chubbies off of her table and snarled, "Where did you get these crayons from?" Lacey, a frigging child, replied, "My mom bought them for me." The teacher ignored the answer and, Chubbies in hand, walked away. She proceeded to ask every white student if the Chubbies belonged to them. At this point, Lacey was crying. The class hadn't even started yet and this woman had made a little girl cry. But Lacey knew redemption was coming. 'Cause when this class was over, she would get to tell Mom. Crayon Karen ended up returning the unclaimed crayons to Lacey (without an apology, of course) and starting her class. Little baby Lacey was fuming mad.

She went home and told Mom what happened and Mom calmly said, "I'll take care of it tomorrow." Now, if you didn't know my mom and you heard her calmly say she'd take care of it tomorrow, you might think she didn't care at all. But what Lacey knew was that Mom was livid and was going to hurt some feelings.

Mom parks the car the next day and walks Lacey into class. Before they walk into the classroom Mom says to Lacey, "Let me see your backpack." Mom proceeds to go up to each staff member and tells them about the items in Lacey's backpack. "This is Lacey, my daughter. These are her crayons. The items she brought with her in this backpack *belong* to her." The first two teachers think, *What an odd thing to say, but do your thing.* When she walks up to the last teacher, Crayon Karen, and says it, the teacher is dumb enough to make the mistake of replying, "Yes. Um... Yes. I see that. We, ummm... We figured that out yesterday." Mom has her idiot. "Did you? Did you get to the bottom of that *mystery*? Well, if you couldn't tell they belonged to Lacey by the fact they were on her desk and came out of her backpack, and she told you so, I thought you would need to hear it from me before you waste everyone's time again by accusing *little girls* of theft." Crayon Karen smartens up and says nothing. She's scared and she should be and it feels good. Mom walks Lacey to her table, watches as she lays out all her stuff, and eyeballs the teachers *hard*. They act right for the rest of the summer.

A lot of these stories end badly, but watching Mom tear into this lady was one of the most satisfying things of all time. Reread it, imagine it vividly, and store it in your mind to replay the next time you're in the mood to watch someone get their comeuppance.

Scary Art Man

In high school, there were two art teachers. A nice one and one that was comically mean. Luckily, Lacey had the nice art teacher. There was so much interest in art that the two art classes would take place next door to each other at the same time. That's right, reader. Public schools used to have art classes! One day, while Lacey is sitting safely in the comfort of her normal art class, the mean teacher bursts in. He walks into Lacey's class, points directly at Lacey, and he says, "You! Come out here right now. Follow me." Lacey is terrified. The mean art teacher has her now. She won't survive much longer. Mean Art Teacher takes her to the front of his completely white class and says to her, "Face the students." He gives a short art lesson using Lacey. He says, "This is the face of the Negro. This is what the negroid race looks like. They have a big nose and full lips. Their skin can be light brown to almost black. When you're drawing a Negro, it should look something like this." Lacey stood there, mortified. "Go back to class now." She walked back to her class in shock.

Can you imagine if that guy had been Lacey's teacher? She'd probably be insane by now! Just kidding. She'd be fine. Every other story in this book is proof!

Jimmy

The gym teacher who we all hated at school also worked at the local bowling alley. We didn't live that far from it, so we would go there to hang out or bowl or have a hot dog. Our brother, Jimmy, absolutely loves video games and would go there to play them as much as he could. One day, Jimmy took a bunch of coins to the bowling alley. Nothing special about the coins. Mostly quarters with some silver dollars or fifty-cent pieces mixed in. When he paid for his food with those coins, Mr. Gym Teacher called the cops. Because he had never seen a silver dollar or a fifty-cent piece, he accused Jimmy of using counterfeit coins.

He accused a child of inventing a special denomination of coin, minting it, and using it to buy hot dogs. When I think about this I wonder, *How in the fuck did this man, the dumbest human being alive, have two jobs?* The kicker is, the cops brought Jimmy home. Jimmy had to cut his time at his favorite place short because some idiot had never seen fifty-cent pieces before and decided to call the cops on a little boy. And, for reasons that include but are not limited to racism, the cops put a child in their car and brought him home instead of telling the idiot gym-teaching cashier that he owed a child an apology.

This book isn't about Jimmy, but I could talk about him all day. Jimmy is a video-game comic-book nerd. Once, in high school, he had left fireworks in his backpack and they were found by the principal or a counselor or whoever that lady was. He had no idea they were in there and wasn't planning on setting them off in school, but it was against the rules to have them there, so the lady sent Jimmy to spend two weeks at a juvenile-delinquent school downtown. Those kids broke Jimmy's collarbone. If this lady knew anything, she would've been able to see that coming. But she didn't because when she looked at Jimmy, she saw someone who belonged at that school instead of the king of nerds and someone who forgot he had fireworks in his backpack. This lady is my friend's mom's friend and I will always, truly, madly, deeply hate her guts. Because—and I don't think this needs to be said—if this were a little white child she was friends with, she would not have sent them there.

The Actually Scary Story

When Lacey was five, she was walking to the grocery store with our two older sisters. On the corner of our street was an old, rundown house. An old man who you almost never saw lived there. It was known as the "old man house." The old man's lawn was crazy overgrown. It had a lot of weeds and vines and stuff and spilled over onto the sidewalk. As they were walking by, our sister Angela's shoe got caught in the weeds, even though she was on the sidewalk. That's how bad his lawn was. Angela bends down to free her shoe from the lawn and re-tie it. The old man sees them and comes outside. He is enraged. He's yelling at them to get off of his property. No one is on his property. They're all on the sidewalk. Angie, even though she's so young. is completely unbothered. Still shouting, the man walks right up to Angie. Angie stands up, toe-to-toe with this old man. He's tiny, so they're about the same size. Angie has both her fists clenched as she looks this screaming old man in the eye. She is waiting for this bitch to make a move. He's a billion years old and has decided to scream at children! But okay. In her face he shouts, "N*****, get your foot off of my lawn!" Again, she is on the sidewalk. Lacey is frozen in fear, but Angie just looks right up at him and says, "Your lawn reached out and grabbed my foot! If you took better care of it, people would be able to walk down the street!" She doesn't budge an inch. She looks at him like, "Feeling froggy, bitch?" Fun fact about Angie: She ain't no punk.

Angie stares this old man down so frigging hard that *he* walks away from *her*! Terrified, they continue to walk to the store. They cross the street and turn the corner so they're still in front of his property, just across the street. The old man is shouting from his yard, following them, shouting, "N*****, go back to where you came from! Go back to where you came from!" Lacey looks at Chrystal, the oldest, and says, "Let's just go home." Chrystal replies, "When he says, 'Go back to where you came from,' that's not what he's talking about." The old man is yelling things like "You don't belong here!" and "You're gonna get in trouble!" Now, it's funny that he thought they didn't belong there. The neighborhood wasn't Black yet, like it is now, but it was browning up pretty nicely at that point. He must've seen the "blackening" of the neighborhood and thought, *I'll scare some kids*. That'll *send a message*!

As they ignore him, the old man, furious that he isn't getting the attention or fear he feels he deserves, goes back into his house and reappears on his porch with a shotgun. He got out a shotgun to defend himself from the five-, eight-, and ten-year-old children who are, at this point, directly across the street. They don't run or scream; they just stand there, staring at him. They may have encountered racism before, but this is something new. A frigging shotgun! A double-barreled shotgun like from the cartoons. Truly a weapon as old as his beliefs. He's shouting, pointing his shotgun, and his wife comes out of the front door crying and screaming for him to come inside. He raises the shotgun, aiming it at them, and his wife keeps pulling down his arm, pleading for him to go back inside. Lacey's not sure why they stood there, or what would've been the best thing to do, but when someone is screaming at you, irate for fun, pointing a gun at you, who knows what the right thing to do is. Lacey is so sure this is their last moment on earth. They stand there for what seems like forever, praying for a miracle, when, out of nowhere, a young African American man pulls up right in front of them and yells, "Get in the car!" They were raised not to talk to strangers, but this, I think, is the mother of all exceptions. They dive in the car without hesitation, and he takes them home. That neighbor with the shotgun lived only four houses away from us. The house has since been demolished. Now it's just an empty lot. If you're wondering why no one called the police, put this book down. You've learned nothing, and this isn't the book for you.

This is just one of the billion crazy racist stories that have happened to Angie. The next book will be all of Angie's stories. There will be no jokes. It will be 1,100 times harsher than most of Lacey's stories. If that's hard for you to imagine, think of the difference between *Hop on Pop* and *Twelve Years a Slave*. You will get four pages in and throw the book out the window. And with Angie's luck, it will hit her right in the head.

SAY HELLO TO CURTIS, THE PALATE-CLEANSING DUCK!

White Church:
The Worst Place on Earth

I am so sorry about this part of the book. These people are real and are probably still at this church. Recently, I saw a headline about one of the pastors who may or may not be mentioned repeatedly in this section. It was an article about how some nutjob pastor said America is safe from coronavirus because Trump is anti-abortion.

My older sisters got invited to a white youth group. That invitation changed their lives.

For many Black teenagers in predominantly white spaces, you begin to ignore the racist things people say. I don't know how to describe this, but you are well aware you live in a racist society. You even know that Omaha is out of the ordinary. You kind of report what is egregious and ignore the less insane. But it is such a regular part of life that you've spent a ton of time just "rolling with it." You're young; you may not even fully understand how or why you're being discriminated against or what you can do about it. Church is the perfect place for crazy racist behavior because your guard is completely down. It's church. Okay, so white church was a bunch of different youth groups gathering from all over the city, from every corner of Omaha. But the church itself is in Bellevue, a city right outside of Omaha. It is whiter than white. So, at this church, Lacey's was the only Black youth group—among the 300 members of the youth group, they stood out. As you read these stories, keep all that in mind and try to remember that in between all these stories are a fun group of Black and white friends who were great, whose friendships have lasted to this day. Let's explore that 1980s small-town dynamic, shall we? Here is a collection of stories from this confusing yet eye-opening time in Lacey's life. How 'bout a fun quote from the pastor of the church to get us started:

> "Music with drums is satanic jungle beats from Africa. It hypnotizes you to make bad decisions."
>
> —Pastor Frank

JENNY

There was a woman named Jenny at this church who was *the* most condescending woman on the planet, one of those white women who truly thought she was "down." Lacey is sitting with a group of white people at church. They're talking about talking on the phone all night, and Jenny turns to Lacey and says, "Lacey, there's this thing on your phone and when you're on a call and a second call comes in, you can just press a button and you can answer the second call. It probably hasn't reached North Omaha yet." This woman was talking about call waiting. At this point it had been years since it was invented, and she is a full dum-dum who doesn't understand how technology works.

She thought advancements in technology are doled out according to race.

She may not have thought you had a phone.

Oh my god.

I know.

If you go out to eat with Lacey, you have to send her the menu ahead of time because it's hard for her to decide what to eat. She's what I call "dinner indecisive." One day, she goes out to eat with Sherri and some others and she's taking forever to decide what to eat. Everyone else is like, "Lacey, can't you decide what you want?" "Hurry up!" Then Jenny comes to Lacey's rescue by saying, "Lacey's probably never been to a place this nice." She turns to one of the guys they're with. "Craig, you're cultured. Why don't you help Lacey by explaining to her what's on the menu? Help her figure out what she wants." Lacey said, "You need to stop talking right now." That restaurant? Olive Garden. The Olive Garden: When You're Here, You're Condescending.

PASTOR FRANK

It was a large white church filled with white people they were invited to on Wednesday nights. It was a fun, youth-group type of place. The music was loud and they played games and it was a cool place to be with a ton of people their age. The church had big buses that picked up all the young folks. My sisters and their friends didn't know they were looked down on at first. They didn't know they came from a place people thought of as bad. Even though the Black kids outdressed them by a mile, the kids at this church still thought the Black kids were dirt poor.

One Wednesday night, a white churchgoer couldn't find her car keys. So Pastor Frank did what any hero would do. He called all of the Black youth group into a room and questioned them, pleading for them to give back the keys. Now, there are 300 people at this church and they don't know who has the keys. No one saw anything. That white woman had not come in contact with the Black kids, yet they were *sure* one of the eight of them had the keys. When the pleading didn't work, they tried a new tactic. Pastor Frank said, "We are gonna turn the lights off and if you have the keys, you can just put them on the table." Pastor Frank and this woman turn the lights out and count to ten. When they turn the lights on again, they look at the table. It is empty and they are disappointed. So they try again. Again there are no car keys on the table. They beg the kids to "do what's right" and reassure them they won't get in trouble. They try again. Nothing. They did this for a good fifteen minutes. The white woman whose car it was was crying. Utterly distraught. "Please, you guys. We know it's one of you who has 'em." This ended with someone coming into the room and saying, "Your keys are locked in your car." It should be said that none of these Black children were even old enough to drive.

Lacey had been a regular at church for quite some time when she was pulled out of the sanctuary and told by Pastor Frank, "Someone said they saw you with a gun." Lacey was confused. "A gun? Where? Why would I have a gun? We're at church! What am I gonna do, shoot Satan?" They made her turn around and asked, "What's in your pocket?" These people who have known Lacey for quite some time and know she's a delight all of a sudden thought she turned to a gun-toting life of crime. What would make them think that? "Why do you think that?" They explained that a white woman who had never come to this church before in her life, whom they had never talked to save for this incident, accused Lacey of having a gun so *of course* they'd have to search her. She turned around and lifted her sweater and showed everyone her comb handle.

Now, if you're asking, "What did they say after these events?" the answer is: not enough. I mean, is there really anything they can say to have any effect on these nutty events? There is not. There is very not.

THE REST OF THESE HEAUX

The church would have different Bible studies at people's houses. This happened all the time, and you got to know everyone. It was fun. This week, Bible study was at Lacey's friend Poppy's house. So everyone is in the living room having Bible study. Lacey walks in and sees a butt-ton of her friends. The living room is filled with white teenagers and Lacey's Bible group of Black teenagers. Poppy's mom sees Lacey's group and says to her daughter, "Poppy, can I see you in the next room, please?" Everyone continues socializing. When Poppy gets back from talking to her mom, she looks distraught. She says to Lacey and her group, "Can I see you guys in the next room, please?" When they meet Poppy in the kitchen, they see Poppy standing there looking ashamed, staring at her feet. She is avoiding eye contact and something is wrong. "My mom says you don't have to leave but you do have to stay in the kitchen. You can eat the snacks, but you can't come in the rest of the house because you weren't invited." She is very embarrassed to have to say this. Now this is where, normally, you would say, "Oh. I'm being treated like shit so I'm out." But this was an impossibility as Poppy was the one who drove them there. That's right: Poppy picked them up and took them to a place they were not invited to. Kinda makes me think they were more than invited, but okay. "We'd rather leave." After seeing the look on everyone's faces, Poppy works up the nerve to go back to her mom and they have it *out*. Everyone can hear it. It's pretty intense. They wonder if they are going to have to leave or if Poppy is going to lose the argument. Poppy comes back into the kitchen holding her car keys. She has lost the argument. She takes them home, apologizing all the way, disgusted with her own mother. No one blamed Poppy; it's clear she wouldn't have taken Black people to her house if she knew she was going to be embarrassed like that. But joke's on Poppy's mom because she married a BLACK GUY. Now, I don't want to encourage you to ever put this book down, but now is a good time to get up, make yourself a drink, and sit back and laugh.

> (Loudly, to the Black kids) "Sit down on your butts!" Then, to her white friend, "That's how you gotta talk to 'em."
> —A white woman from church

> "When I do my ministry in North Omaha, I make sure I have my gun."
> —One of the white pastors

Back to Pastor Frank. He drove an old Firebird or something along those lines. An old car that he liked for some reason but was a true piece of shit. Like, if you're a car guy, maybe you could be proud of it. But if you're a regular person, you'll apologize for the fact that people have to look at it. The kids would look at it and laugh because it was a hot mess of a car. Frank would say stuff like "One day I hope that you guys have a car as nice as this. And one day I pray that you will move out of North Omaha into a nice place." He said that as if all of North Omaha was bad instead of it being a giant section of Omaha with great and not-so-great neighborhoods. Keep in mind that our parents live in a three-bedroom, three-bathroom house that sits on an acre and a third. Our folks are doing just fine. Pastor Frank lived in a very not-so-great neighborhood in South Omaha in an apartment he shared with three other guys. So this guy really thought he was out here doing frigging missionary work, when he should've been trying to scam a home-cooked meal off of one of our parents.

Lacey's twelve. Someone from church comes up to her and says, "Hey, you're from North Omaha! What side are you on?" Lacey replies, "I don't know, the north side?" He says, "No, Crip or Blood?"

I said Blood and stabbed him.

She did not.

I could have.

That is true.

When Bill Clinton was elected, one of the white pastors stood up and said that it was a sin to vote for Bill Clinton and if you did, you needed to come to the altar and repent. And some people DID! I laugh every time I hear that story. Nuts, man.

There was a big youth group meeting with, like, fifty people at it. All the Black kids were there. For those keeping count, that's eight Black kids and forty-two white people. They made an announcement. "White women should not come to North Omaha because gang members are being initiated." Now there's nothing I can say to prepare you for what I'm about to tell you. I need you to take a deep breath before you read the rest of this story. Maybe take a minute to think about the fact that "North Omaha" is massive and mostly white. It's also where a lot of the Black people are. Are you prepared yet? One more deep breath. These white people were truly insane. Lord knows how this happened, but this grown man said, "White women should not come to North Omaha because gang members are being initiated. And the way you get initiated into the gangs is by cutting off white women's clitorises." Flip the page and leave those feelings here.

A Black man and a white woman got married at white church and, after the wedding, she told everyone jokingly, "My wedding certificate is like slave documents because I own this Negro now and if he acts up, I'll just whip him!" Everyone, including this man, laughed. Y'all, the joy with which she made this joke truly makes me think this is why she married him. They must have some fucked-up kids by now.

Ryan Prute

The North Omaha Bible study group was invited to a small town in Iowa for a retreat. A retreat is typically where your church meets up with a bunch of other churches and goes to a campsite with a few cabins and has church in a new place. Everyone sings songs around a campfire and eats bad food. Dad hears this and is like, "Go if you want, but I am not driving out there to pick you up." My dad is a smart Black adult. He knows that this reeks of a bad idea. But there was going to be a speaker there and all the other kids were going, so he let us go. We arrive and it was all white people. We're a little sad, but what are you gonna do? Then we see that the speaker is a Black man! Finally! These idiots will get to see an example of a real Black man instead of the insane stereotypes these people are walking around with that me and my friends can't seem to put a dent in. Joy of joys! This is an excellent opportunity for some of the racist people that go to this church to get rid of some of the horrible stereotypes they believe and see us for who we really are. We are thrilled. Now, this retreat is a whole weekend and we still have these white children to deal with, so we calm it down. We choose places to sleep and as we do, we meet a bunch of white children from Bum-fuck, Iowa. These are children who have never seen a Black person in their entire lives. We're scared that it will go poorly, but these kids take to our North Omaha group and it's a relief. We all giggle and laugh and decide to bunk together. As everyone picks places to sleep, they throw their bags willy-nilly together with ours as we claim a room in Cabin A. We all rush to the big auditorium! It's time to hear the speaker! Dad was wrong. We're gonna make new friends and memories to last a lifetime! Friendship!

This group of eight Black kids are so proud of this Black speaker that we walk all the way up to the front of the auditorium to sit in the very front row. We're beaming with pride as this man starts his speech. He speaks about "inner-city Black youth." Okaayyyy. He was talking about it as us versus them. And he was the "us." We were the "them." It was unbelievable fearmongering like you have never seen in your life. Not from a Black person about Black people, not from a white person about Black people. No one— no one—has publicly said things like this in the presence of Black people. Here are some points he made about Black people:

These people will try to rob you.

They'll try to kill you.

They're a drain on the economy.

He talks about every last stereotype.

Then he kind of riles himself up with disgust for Black people, saying, "They don't care; they're rude. Once, I was at a restaurant and I saw a Black kid walk through a door and not hold it open for an old white lady. The kid just slammed the door shut! Can you believe it? Did you not see there was a human being here? There's no respect in the Black community for PEOPLE!" This man is now visibly upset. It becomes a fire-and-brimstone sermon, but its only topic is Black people and how bad we are. This man recites Black stereotypes for the next hour and a half.

At the end of his speech, we are embarrassed and ashamed of this man. But we also see why he is so popular. We look around at the people we came here with. They look like they've just heard the juiciest secret of their whole lives. White people ate this shit up! It confirmed all of their deepest, darkest, most racist beliefs. Suddenly they were justified in treating Black people like crap.

Dang.

Right afterward, we get up and walk up to Ryan and tell him how his sermon made us feel. I will never forget his reply. He rolled his eyes and said, "Hey, this message wasn't *for* you. I don't even know why you guys were here."

We got up, went back to our room in shock. We looked around, and the white people who were our new best friends two hours ago were scrambling to grab all of their stuff and move as far away from us as possible. We called Dad. He came to get us.

Amber Ruins the Book

THE COPS: THEY'RE A RIOT!
JUST KIDDING—THEY'RE DANGEROUS AND
UNNECESSARILY LETHAL

The whole point of this book is to tell you a bunch of Lacey's stories and have everyone see how crazy they are. But we have to take a break from that for a second. I could not write a book about racism and not include a section about cops. Specifically *me* and cops. So for the next teeny little bit, indulge me and pretend you're reading a slightly more serious book. Maybe it's called something like *A Troubled Nation*. Or it's an essay called "The Dangers of Overpolicing."

I used to live in Chicago! It was a very fun time in my life when I was the least aware of the world, yet most independent. I took improv classes and interned at a theater and made new friends every day. I lived right down the alley from a police station. My neighborhood (Boystown) was pretty darn white, which, when you're Black, doesn't make you feel safe. Here's why!

I lived in one of those houses that had three apartments in

it. Every once in a while, I would enter my house from the alley instead of the front. My bedroom looked out on the alley and oftentimes I could spy people making out or straight-up getting nasty. One night, my friend Tony (a Black guy) was leaving my apartment. He hopped on his bike and rode off but had left his wallet. I didn't realize this 'til I had changed into pajamas. I called him, he came back, I stepped out, shoeless, onto the back stairs and reached down and handed him his wallet. He dropped his bike and walked over to me. Sirens went off. "What are you doing? What's going on over there! Hold it right there!" The cop had Tony put his hands on the hood of the car while she patted him down. I explained that he was just here and I live here. She demanded to see both our IDs. We showed them to her. Now this woman is mad. A lot of the time, when you deal with cops, it's not only your job to do what they say, it's your job to de-escalate the situation. A lot of these cops come at you at a ten and if you want to survive the interaction, you gotta get 'em down to a six. This woman was at an eight. She runs our IDs and comes back and is still mad. I tell her that I live here. I'm on the back stairs in pajamas and no frigging shoes, for fuck's sake. She makes me go inside and get a piece of mail with my name on it. Now, this woman has stopped us for no reason, frisked Tony, run our IDs, and we have literally done nothing wrong. We were in an alley after dark. She explains to us that Tony was running away from her police car. He ditched his bike to get away from them. He was trying to come into my house before they heroically stopped him. I mean, dude.

Many years later, after I had moved to Amsterdam, I came back to Chicago to visit. I'm on my way to pick up my friend Krazny who lived next door to me in police station alley. Our friend parks at the gas station at the end of the alley so I can run up and get her. I'm frigging thrilled. I hadn't seen her in years and we were on our way to have dinner and catch up. Because he is watching me, I skip down the alley to her house. But little did I know, skipping down police station alley is a big no-no. I end up skipping toward a cop car driving down the alley. The sirens go off. A cop gets out and his gun is drawn. "Put your hands on the hood of the car! Put your hands on the hood. Now!" I think it is safe to say that this man is at a ten. I comply and he pats me down and is livid. It is as if he had just seen me punch a child in the face. This man's anger level toward me is insane. I'm a young, adorable delight literally skipping down the street and I've infuriated him.

"Where are you coming from?"

"Amsterdam." This answer enrages him.

"No! Where are you coming from right now!"

"From the airport. From a flight. From Amsterdam."

"Why in the world are you running down this alley?"

"I'm not running. I'm skipping. I'm happy to be back in town. I'm going to pick up my friend Krazny and take her back to Jeff's car. We are all gonna go catch up over dinner." I gesture back to Jeff and he's standing outside of his car at the gas station at the end of the alley watching all of this. He waves. Thank god he didn't come running up to us. He'd have gotten both of us shot. The cop sees that Jeff, a white man, has seen all this and he changes his attitude with the quickness. He tells me not to run in the alley. It takes everything in me not to tell him that if I wanted to run in the alley, that would be perfectly legal. I instead oh-so-gently remind him I was skipping. The cop gets in his car and leaves. I walk away to Krazny's house. Jeff is really bothered by what has happened. I'm not. Shit, that man could have shot me in a second. People who know me would be running around talking about "Attacking an officer doesn't *sound* like something she'd do, but the officer said that's what happened. So I guess that's what happened!" The second I see my friend, I feel a lot better. We go out and have a lot of fun that night. It's kind of my duty to have fun, if you really think about it. 'Cause at any time, I could get murdered by the police.

My first encounter with the police was in Council Bluffs, Iowa. It's a city just over the river from Omaha. Black people in Omaha always say that our cops are bad but in Council Bluffs, they're way worse. So I drop off my friend at work in Council Bluffs one morning. I've only been driving for like a year and I'm in the middle of a lot of morning traffic. It's, I think, one of those streets that has three lanes both ways. It's the main street that goes all the way through Council Bluffs to Omaha. So I notice that we are all going over the speed limit. I think it's forty, and everyone is going fifty. I hate it. But when I slow down, it disrupts traffic. So I go forty-five. It's only five miles over the limit and it's the fastest I'm willing to go. I'm too new to driving and I'm in Council Bluffs. I'm not really familiar with this place. To make myself feel better, I turn on Busta Rhymes. I blast it. Blasting Busta Rhymes is something I recommend if you're nineteen and unsure of yourself. So I get used to the pace and start to feel okay driving at this speed. Just then, I encounter a speed trap. No one slows down. We are all speeding. I look to my right and there's an old white cop standing on the side of the road. Out of these tens of cars, he hears my loud music and sees a Black person driving and chooses me. He's screaming right at me. If the last guy was at a ten, this man is at a twenty-seven.

"Pull over! Pull the goddamn car over right now, motherfucker!" That is what this old white cop screams at me during my first solo drive in Council Bluffs. This is how I die. This man is going to kill me. I start crying. I pull over as this man continues his obscenity-laden tirade. It is venomous. He's disgusted with me. "Pull over the fucking car!" He walks up to my car and sees the state I'm in. I'm a nineteen-year-old girl and I look terrified. My whole face is wet with tears and I'm trying to remember all the good things that have happened to me in life so I can get to heaven thankful instead of angry. He looks at me and I am not what he is expecting to see. He is taken aback. He goes from a twenty-seven to a negative-two. His whole demeanor changes. "Okay. All right. It's okay. Let's just see your license. Okay? Can you do that?" This guy sounds like Mister Rogers. He lets me off with a warning and is so sweet and so kind to me I cannot believe it is the same man. He's telling me, "You're all right. Everything's fine." As if he wasn't just screaming at me. I am so thankful. Not in that moment, but now. I think what happened was he couldn't quite see me. From far away, this cop thought I was a Black man, and he was ready to drag me out of the car and beat the crap out of me. Once he saw I was a young woman, that was less appealing. It was maybe the single most important life lesson I'll ever learn. Racist people have Black friends, they love Black people, and even protect some Black people. The same cops that would happily beat a Black man to death would catch pneumonia looking for a lost little Black girl all night in the woods. It doesn't make them less guilty or better human beings. It makes them deceitful little pieces of shit and I swear to god I have no patience for someone who has sworn to protect people beating people to death for fun.

Oh my god, this is not what this book is.

I know, but once I get going.

Once she gets going it's hard to stop her. Stop.

You are right. I will stop. Just know, that's not the end of my cop stories.

You guys aren't gonna hear most of my cop stories. There's just not enough room! Amber, you've ruined the vibe. Here, guys. A non–race related palate cleanser:

Here's why I'm afraid of butterflies: When I was little I had a very fluffy pink sweater. It had a cursive letter *L* on it like Laverne's from *Laverne & Shirley*. I loved that sweater and wore it as often as I could. One day when I was about seven years old, I was at the neighbor's house and a butterfly landed on my fluffy sweater. It was cute. My friends gathered around me and looked at it. Fun. We went back to playing, but the butterfly wouldn't fly away. I shook my sweater—nothing. I put my hand underneath my sweater and tried to shake it loose—nothing. So I had to resort to gently wiping it away. He was so tangled in the fluffiness of the sweater that when I did, the wings popped off and just the body remained. A butterfly with wings is vastly different from one without. I looked down and saw a gross, long, half-smashed, tangled-up bug body and screamed. I took off my shirt and ran home topless.

No! This is the non–race related palate cleanser you shoulda told. It would be called: Lacey's white stalker and how she couldn't bring herself to be afraid of him.

Ha ha ha. Yes.

Here's a story that has nothing to do with race, although this man was white. In a high-end boutique Lacey was working at, a white man walked in on a very hot July day wearing a trench coat. What made Lacey remember what he was wearing is that Mom had the exact same trench coat. It was lavender and iridescent. Beautiful. Maybe in my top ten coats of all time. I hope Mom still has it. If she does, we will take a picture in it and put it right here. If she doesn't, close your eyes and imagine heaven in a coat. It was spectacular. So this man walks in in my mom's coat and he looks like a beautiful princess. He has long blond hair and is, like, six-five. He's super tall. So at first glance, it seems like they're gonna get along great. But then, Lacey could tell he seemed very nervous. He was acting strangely. Lacey assumed it was because he was planning on stealing something. So she walked up to him and started a conversation in hopes that would deter him from stealing. It did. He told Lacey his life story. It took thirty minutes. This man has traveled the world as a natural healer. He's had many adventures. Lacey nods and listens. This man is yapping his boring little butt off, but it is better than him stealing. That's when things took a turn. He began telling Lacey he loved her Black skin, asking if she's single. Uh-oh. He loved how her skin looked and wanted to caress it. Too far. Lacey told him to leave or she was gonna have to call security. The second she said "security," he said bye and left. Why? Why must creepiness come from every-where? The last thing Lacey expected from this man was him hitting on her, but okay, whatever. He's gone now. As soon as he leaves, Lacey notices two white women waving hysterically from the store across the way. She had seen them before during opening and closing time. They also work in the shopping center. They ran over and said, "That guy you were talking to just stole from our stores! He just stole a bunch of high heels and put them in his trench coat." Lacey is shocked. "The guy you just watched me talk to for thirty minutes? Why didn't you call security?" These women replied, "We thought he was your friend. And we didn't want you to get mad at us." They thought the thief was Lacey's friend. Of course they did. Later, Lacey found out they thought she was in on it. Lacey calmly tells them, "When someone steals, you always call security. You don't wait to see who they steal from next. You just call security. Always call security." Lacey thinks that this is just a one-off odd event and chalks it up to the fact that "people crazy."

Trench Coat Man comes back in about a week or so. Lacey's not working but the biggest idiot in the world is. Let's call him TBIITW. Trench Coat asks the biggest idiot in the world, TBIITW, for Lacey's name. He gives it to him. Trench Coat asks when Lacey will be working next; TBIITW tells him. Trench Coat asks for her address and phone number; TBIITW says, "Whoa. Wait a second. Are you gonna stalk Lacey?" Just kidding. He's the biggest idiot in the world! Of course, he gives him the info, no questions asked!

And so it begins. After that Lacey received phone calls and love letters. He would even try to come into the store and talk to Lacey, even though every time she would immediately tell him to leave and call security. The whole while in Mom's beautiful trench coat. This went on for quite some time. After Lacey had gotten a new job, the boss said Trench Coat had dropped off a letter for Lacey. Here's the letter:

From This Day Forward

May the hounds of hell be always on your ass!
May you dream of dogs as they chew your face off!
May you suffocate while a 450lb maggot infested woman sits on your face with the screaming acid shits !
You will here voices when you walk and when you turn around. You will see only Death on your trail!
May the Reaper take you to hell before your time!
Yea , as I walk through the valley in the the shadow of death, I will fear no evil.For I be the deadliest mother fucker in the valley!

Lacey takes the letter to the cops. The police try to let her know she should be scared. Maybe they had a point, but I know Lacey. That man should be scared. They started a file on the guy, but Lacey never knew his real name, so she could never file a restraining order. This man sends Lacey more love letters because their "souls are connected." He tries to get in touch with her for the next year. Lacey then realizes that this man is the best she can do so she gives in to love.

Amber.

I lied. She makes sure to tell everyone about him in case they see him. She doesn't feel scared of this guy at all, but he sure is bothering her a whole bunch. So, one day, Lacey is working out at a really nice gym she was a member of. You can't come in there unless you are a member. You need a key fob that brings up a picture of you, they check it against your actual face, and then they buzz you in. Even Lacey has to do that every time, and she's friends with the manager. If you're not a member, how could you possibly get in? She is on the treadmill and looks to her left and there's Trench Coat. She immediately gets off the treadmill and walks right up to the manager and says, "This man has been stalking me for years. Can I have his name so I can file a restraining order?" The manager says, "I'll give you whatever you want." This is it! She's finally gonna get that restraining order! There's no way this guy got in there without some ID. The manager says to the receptionist, "Pull all his info." The receptionist says, "What's wrong?" The manager says, "We need this guy's info." The receptionist says, "He didn't show any ID. He was wearing a suit and had a gym bag. I assumed he was a member!" This stalker just used his whiteness to saunter in. Must be nice. Trench Coat notices three people standing around and talking about him. He makes a run for it. The manager stops him and says, "Are you a member? Give me your name."

Trench Coat simply walks out and says, "No." The end. Lacey never sees him again. If you're keeping score, it's:

Lacey—none
Whiteness—a million

Someone once asked me, "Why didn't you follow him out to his car?" I mean, I'm not scared but I'm also not stupid.

Oh my god! I said it wasn't but this did end up being a story about race!

That's right! Because he never could have walked into the gym with no ID or anything without being white. He never could have gotten all my information from my coworker without being white. Boy. Just when you think you've escaped it.

You can't escape it. Back to fun[1] stories!

---

1   This cannot be how you're supposed to use the word *fun*.

I Want to Put This Book Down
and Run Away from It

D on't do what the chapter title says to do. You made it this far and I'm truly proud of you. I've assembled these stories together in this chapter because each of these stories is perfect. Like, if these each were little short stories you wrote, you'd get an A. (Your teacher would be concerned, but you'd get an A.) They're not the most racist stories in this book, but they are technically harder to believe because they are so beautiful. Except beautiful means ugly because we are talking about racism.

I hope you're enjoying yourself and laughing and learning and living and loving. Speaking of loving, in this chapter we're gonna talk about being in an interracial couple! (Google it—that was a good joke.) We're also going to tell you my two favorite stories.

RACIST DOUGHNUTS

Lacey used to work in a small town in Nebraska. It was not the best job, it was a terrible commute, and she once again was the only Black person in the entire place. But it made her money that she used to live, so it met her requirements. It was a regular office job at an old folks' home. She organized parties and wrote up expense reports. A pretty boring job. One day, some of her coworkers breezed through with the most important announcement you can make in an office: "Doughnuts!" And, upon hearing that, like any red-blooded American, she sprinted to the kitchen faster than Jackie Joyner-Kersee.[1]

She gets to the office kitchen and there is a full box of doughnuts. They look great. She takes one. And to clarify, this is Nebraska. We don't get office doughnuts and cut them into several pieces and pass them out like cartoon orphans. You grab a whole doughnut because you're a grown-ass woman. She takes a bite out of this doughnut and loves it.

Amber, I fear you're not getting across just how delicious these doughnuts are. I take a bite of this doughnut and am immediately sent to heaven. Not like I'm dead, but, if I had died in that moment, I would have been okay with that. It was the most delicious doughnut any human being has ever eaten. Sweet and fluffy. After you finish this book, please buy my second book, *The Doughnut I Ate*—available in my heart.

We get it! The doughnut was great. Anyway, there at that crappy job with those well-meaning but ultimately shitty people, she

---

1   Faster than Flo-Jo? Usain Bolt? Which sprinters are you familiar with? Please email me your answers at getonwithit@shutup.com.

enjoyed the butt off that doughnut. How many did you have, Lacey?

How many I ate is not what this story is about, so I need you to lay off me. Even if, throughout the day, I ate four, a totally reasonable number of doughnuts, I need you to try to focus on the story.

Okay. She had four great doughnuts. Later that week, another miracle occurred. They hired a SECOND BLACK WOMAN! The two of them locked eyes and, in a single gaze, shared the relief of seeing each other, the "ain't that about a bitch" of it all, and the agreement that they would have a secret meeting later. When they did, Lacey learned that she (let's call her Tish, which could be her name for all Lacey knows because she can't remember it to save her doughnut-loving life) was expecting these new employers to treat her like any normal employer would. She was young, smart, and expecting fair treatment. Lacey envied her and simultaneously wondered what on earth would make her think that a small town in the middle of Nebraska was where she was going to find that. Lacey knew Tish wouldn't last long at this job. These people were going to say something perfectly racist to her. She was going to give them a piece of her mind, storm out, and never come back. Before she inevitably quit, Tish would need to taste the doughnuts.

Lacey asked her coworkers where they got the doughnuts and they gave her directions. "It's kind of hard to find." The next day, she stopped by the place before she went into work. She left home way too early because not only did she have to pay her rent that morning, she is prone to getting lost. But, miracle of miracles, she didn't get lost that morning. After paying the rent, she drove straight to the little dough-nut shop.

If Lacey's life were a movie, and it is, and you were watch-ing it, and you kind of are, when you saw her going into this doughnut shop you would yell, "No! Don't! They'll kill you!"

This place was a frigging gross shack with a tin roof, almost falling apart. She didn't care. She's getting her doughnuts. On the inside was a regular doughnut shop case and small counter and register. There was a weird kitchen table with three chairs at it, each of them from a different decade. She went in with a big smile on her face, determined to be polite. And it was a good thing, too, because the women behind the counter glared at her like Lacey glared at the outside of their building. I'm not saying a person can "look" racist, but Lacey is. She said that. Can you believe her?

I said that. It's like, you know how women know when a man is scary? It's like a lifetime of survival skills kick in and you get a bit of a spidey sense about some situations? Well, I've been in approximately a billion racist situations. So I know. From the "Black people have dumb names" kind of racists to the "only ever talk to you about music" type of racists. My spidey sense is strong. Now, I can't tell when everyone's racist, but when I think someone's a racist, they are. And I'm saying these people were racist.

This is how their transaction went:
   Lacey: Good morning!

These 2 women (angrily): What.

Lacey (chipper as heck): I'd like a dozen doughnuts, please.

Meany and Meaner: They're not ready yet. You would have to wait.

Lacey: Not a problem!

It's eight in the morning; you are a doughnut shop. We all know darn well the doughnuts are ready but, hey, let's do it. The two doughnut heauxs roll their eyes and mutter to each other. They think they're being mean enough to Lacey to get her to leave. They are not. In fact, compared to her job, this is the frigging ACLU. She goes and stands against the wall and plays on her phone. Five minutes turn into ten turn into fifteen, and she's chillin' like a mug. She has a full phone battery and all the time in the world.

I also have a purpose. Tish *must* taste the doughnuts. She drove all the way in from Omaha and probably doesn't have very long at this job. I'm determined to have *one* good thing happen to her.

An old man comes in. Hoo boy, does he not like that Lacey's in there. He orders his whatever and then walks over to her. The two women behind the counter are watching as he barks at her, "That's *my* seat." Mind you, Lacey is not sitting in a seat. She is standing against the wall. But she's standing too close to his seat for his liking. Now, this is how they try to get you. Racist people will say mean things to you to start a fight, then call the cops and then play the victim. Tale as old as time. But today is about getting dough-nuts for her new friend, Tish, so she doesn't leave this job without knowing true doughnut love, not exacting revenge. She chirps back, "Great!" but doesn't move a single inch. Her reasons for not budging are twofold. One, this man is a ninety-year-old raggedy bitch who barely made it to the counter. And two, these women aren't going to like that she's making their friend uncomfortable and that will make them get her doughnuts faster. And it worked, because almost immediately:

The doughnut coven: "Don't you want your doughnuts?"

Lacey, the hero of this story, handing them her credit card: "Here you go!"

A supergross smirk creeps across their faces. "We don't take credit cards."

Lacey is disappointed.

Disappointed is not the word. Devastated is more like it. I said out loud, "Oh dear god, no." I check my wallet and I have no cash. I cannot believe it. It can't end like this. I am defeated. I waited all this time for absolutely nothing. How could I have let this happen? They win. The racists win. I will not be getting my doughnuts today.

As they all but celebrate, Lacey asks, "Do you take checks?"

The smiles drop from their faces and they reply, "Yes." They scan my face to see whether or not their answer matters. But, you guys, I go out to my car and pull the checkbook from the glove box. I JUST SO HAPPENED TO HAVE MY CHECKBOOK 'CAUSE I HAD JUST PAID RENT! And it's at this point that I'd like to point out how stupid racists are.

Why didn't they just say, "No. We don't take checks"? I have no way of knowing if they take checks or not. Also, who the fuck still takes checks? What year is it?

She cuts these pieces of shit a check, and, victorious, goes back to work.

She finds Tish and tells her the story. Tish is disgusted that she would spend any money at such a racist place. "How could you give them your business? Why didn't you just leave?"

And, I have to say, she is right. I do have to say I normally would not have given them my business but there was something about seeing these racists so uncomfortable. But also, these doughnuts are fantastic, sooooo . . .

"I'm not giving a racist store my business." Tish leaves the office kitchen without taking a single doughnut. That bums Lacey out. She did this for her. The only thing that could console Lacey at this point would be four doughnuts. And they did.

Later in the day, Tish comes bursting into Lacey's office with a doughnut in hand. She had seen everyone's joyful, doughnut-eating faces and caved. "Lacey, you were right! These are delicious! They're the best doughnuts I've ever had!"

"I know."

They laugh and right before Tish leaves, she says, "I'll pick up the doughnuts next time."

There is no next time. That week, the boss tells Tish her clothes are too tight, and she tries to explain the concept of "policing Black women's bodies." It does not go over well. She quits.

THE DOLL

Lacey used to be the program director at a retirement home. It was fun and the people weren't racist at all. Just kidding. It was hilariously racist and she looked for another job every single day. This retirement home was designed to look like a cruise ship and when you first come in the door, there's a big gift shop with stuff old people like. Magnets, wind chimes, dolls, stuff like that. One day, Lacey notices that among the lily-white dolls is a new Black one. It's right in the center of the store. You can't miss it when you walk in, both because for some reason this gift shop thinks these dolls are the prized jewel of their stock and also because one Black face always stands out. We all know no one is ever going to buy that doll because there are no Black people in the home and, even if there were, they're probably not gonna want a doll.

As time goes on, different employees take turns going, "There's a doll that looks just like you, Lacey!" Now, there's only one Black doll. We all know which one they're talking about. Also, Lacey does not look anything like that doll. And there are a lot of baby dolls that she looks ***exactly*** like (it's the forehead). But this one ain't it. Everyone has something to say:

"You left your baby in the gift shop!"
"Hey, Big Lacey, I just saw Little Lacey!"

"Didn't I just see you in the gift shop? How'd you get here so fast?"

That one's actually not bad.

With each dumb comment, Lacey grows to hate this doll. Every time she passes by the store, she can't help but look at it and think, *No one is telling all you white people you look like these shitty dolls. And you actually DO!* So she gets sick of Black Doll Jokes (tm) and does what any normal person would do: she puts the doll in the back of the gift shop so it's not the first thing you see as you walk by. The jokes slow down and, aside from everything else, it gets better.

After a while at this job, Lacey finally finds another place to work. She gives her supervisor her resignation. She's sad to lose Lacey. But she tells her to not make any decisions until tomorrow. Lacey says okay even though there is nothing on earth that could keep her at this job.

The next morning she comes in and you already know what she finds on her desk: that motherfucking doll. Along with the doll is a card that says, "There's always a way." Her boss thought the doll that she hates would make her realize that she needs to stay with them. That she could not have bought the damn thing for herself. That her buying it meant she really knew what Lacey liked. That she would feel appreciated. She comes into Lacey's office talking 'bout some "Here you go, Lacey! Bet you don't want to leave us now, huh?"

I want to slap her in the mouth, but instead I say, "Thank you. My resignation stands."

This doll remained hilarious in our family until we realized it looks exactly like our niece! Now the doll is the funniest thing that has ever happened.

YOUR H-H-H-HUSBAND IS W-W-W-WHITE?

Lacey's white then husband, Jim, left his ID at a bank. On her way home, she picked it up for him. At this point in the book, I hope I don't need to tell you it was difficult.

She went into the bank, walked up to the teller.

Lacey: Hi, there. My husband left his ID here today. I'm wondering if you could check your lost-and-found for me?

Teller Lady: Of course! Don't you worry. This happens all the time! My husband is real forgetful, too! What would they do without us?

Lacey: Nothing, because they'd be lost!

The two share a laugh.

Lacey gives her his first and last name. This woman picks up a small box with a bunch of IDs in it. She looks through the box. "Sorry, I don't see it." Lacey repeats his name. She looks through the box again. As she's looking through all the IDs, Lacey can see Jim's ID. "It's not in here." Lacey repeats his name again and watches Teller Lady look through them. This time, Lacey realizes, the teller is not looking at the names, she's looking for a Black man, and there are none. She has her search one more time for fun before she tells her, "It's right there." The teller replies, "Your husband is white? How in the world do you get along?"

You guys. Y'all. You guys. People. This woman asked, "How in the world do you get along?" I'd love to say I said some great eye-opening smart remark but, frankly, that shocked me. I hadn't heard that one before. "How in the world do you get along?" Wow. It's bad when it comes out of nowhere, but it's also pretty bad when you know darn well you're dealing with a racist person from the get-go.

Yes! Like, for example, Lacey's apartment hunting with Jim. They were meeting at an apartment building in a perfectly normal neighborhood. Not very fancy. Not very much of anything. A fine place to live. Jim lets her know he's gonna be late, so Lacey goes ahead in, alone.

As soon as she walks into the office, she can see that the man behind the desk wishes she hadn't. But that won't stop Lacey from being her nicest! It has been a happy day so far, and once this guy sees what a good time Lacey is, she is certain this guy will come around.

"Hello there! I was wondering if you have any—"

"We don't got nothing."

The man was mean and slightly angry. There are all kinds of racism. Most people are racist in a quiet way or a scared way, but some folks are racist in a "How dare you be Black at me" way. I've never fully understood it, but this guy was one of those. Lacey turns away and goes back to the car, 'cause she has a plan. Jim shows up.

Lacey: The guy in the leasing office was so rude to me! I got a feeling he does have apartments but just didn't want to show them to me because I'm Black.

Jim: Great. Let me go in there and hurt his feelings.

Lacey: No. Go in, be normal, and see if they have apartments.

So he goes in there. He's gone for a good ten minutes and when he gets back, he tells Lacey that the man could not have been nicer to him. He told him, "We got a bunch of available stuff." He even showed him a place.

After Jim reports back to her, she busts back in the office with him and says, "This is my husband, you raggedy racist! Trust that you will be hearing from our lawyer. I hope you didn't like this job." The guy gets fired and the apartment complex offers them a place at a discount. They decline.

GONE BABY GONE

At what might be the most racist job of all time, Lacey actually got to work at the same place as a few Black people. Yay! This place is ninety percent Black staff/ninety-nine percent white directors. There are a lot of Black nursing assistants who work with the residents. All staff, from directors on down, sometimes bring their kids to work! The residents love it, and it's a regular occurrence. And on this day, a Black CNA, let's call her Nala, gets permission to bring her child to work. This child, like many others, has been to work before. She is a cute little three-year-old girl, perhaps as well behaved as a three-year-old can be. At the beginning of Nala's shift, a white supervisor comes out of her office and says, "Oh! I can take your daughter into my office while you finish your work." Nala takes her up on it and says, "Thank you!"

Now, this white supervisor is a nosy nancy in a very bad way. She's privileged, and can't understand the community she works in. The climate of this building is racist to the following degree:

I found out later that while she was gone, a few of the CNAs saw the white supervisor loudly reprimanding the baby and "snatching her up."

Nala returns to check on her kid in under an hour. And when she does, the office is shut, locked, and empty. Now, this facility is huge. It's the size of three large apartment buildings put together, so where do you even begin to look for a three-year-old? Nala makes her way through one building, then through the next. This search takes two hours.

That is two hours too long. Can you imagine not being able to find your child for two hours?

No. I don't have children.

Okay. Can you imagine not being able to find your margarita for two hours?

I would die.

Exactly.

Meanwhile, in baby jail, the white supervisors and a few shit stirrers decide the baby has a mysterious bruise. As a result, they call CPS and 911.

Now, this is the part of the story that sounds wholly unmotivated and impossible to believe. Why would this lady call the COPS on a mom for absolutely no reason? But remember what racism is? It makes reasonable people insane.

When Nala comes around the corner yelling, "Somebody better tell me where my baby is!" the police see her and instantly know who she is. "Ma'am, come with us. We know where your baby is." They take her to a room containing her baby and four white people, all directors. They let her know the deal. They think there's a bruise on this baby and have called CPS. This woman stands there and calmly says, "They've had my baby for almost two hours. Two hours ago, the baby had no bruises." The police take the baby from the boss and hand her to the mother. Luckily, the police agreed with the mom and said, "We don't know where this bruise came from." I am ashamed of myself when I think about how happy I am that this lady didn't get her baby taken away. But I can't help it. This lady could have lost her child because these people were bored. These people kidnapped a baby, bruised her, and called the cops on the mother. Let's tell this tale differently:

Four Black people take a white child in a room and hide her for two hours from her white mother. Maaaaan.

There's Nothing I Can Say to You to Make You Believe These Stories, but Here They Are Anyway

You made it. You made it to the last chapter of the book. These are stories that I feel are extreme for any number of reasons. Some because they are so structurally perfect and some because they're so brutal. So let's finish this book off with a potpourri of racist nonsense!

Lacey was with a coworker, let's call her Buttface. Just kidding. Let's call her Vanessa. I've always liked that name. Okay, so, Vanessa, who just so happens to be a buttface, and Lacey have to pick up supplies for a party at the retirement home. There is a party supply store not too far away. It's the one Lacey always goes to. It's BARELY in a Black neighborhood. Vanessa flat-out refuses to go. "It's in North Omaha and it's too dirty! I don't want to go to a dirty store!" Guys, there's nothing wrong with this store. It's perfect. Lacey has been there a million times and, even though she loves a deal, she does not do dirt. Also, Vanessa has never been to this store. She only doesn't want to go because she thinks Black people will be there. That's the level of buttface we are dealing with here. But, okay, if you wanna go somewhere else, fine. Looking on the bright side, she's not going to be around any Black people saying crazy racist things, so that's a plus. And she's driving, so who gives a rip! Lacey assures her she is wrong and agrees to go to her store. This woman proceeds to drive to her store. Now, it rarely takes more than twenty minutes to get anywhere in Omaha. But Vanessa gets on the interstate and drives for a while. After a while, Lacey asks, "Where are you going?" This woman replies, "A great store in Iowa!" Iowa. That is a different state. She would drive to a different state rather than just go to a store in North Omaha? Okay. This store better be good.

Y'all. You guys. People. Folks. Y'all. You're not gonna believe it. You know how earlier when you read the phrase *dirty store* you thought, *That's odd. Stores can be cluttered or low quality, but not* dirty. Man, I thought the same thing 'til Lacey showed me a picture of this Iowa travesty. This store was comically dirty. Cluttered? Yes. Disorganized? Yes. But also full of *actual* dust and dirt on the floor and on the merchandise. Lacey was shocked. So shocked that she took pictures of the stores so you could see for yourself.

Here's the North Omaha store:

And here's the Iowa store:

One October, everyone at work is discussing Halloween costumes. It's a really rare, nice conversation where everyone is talking about making bunny ears or how to paint your face like a cat, and Lacey is appreciating it. Fun fact about Lacey and me: We love holiday dress-up! Red on Valentine's, green on Saint Patrick's Day, and shoulder pads on Anita Baker's[1] birthday! There was even a thing in Omaha called River City Roundup where you would come to school dressed like cowboys. It was the cutest day of the year. Anyhoo, they have such a nice time in their conversation that they decide to dress up for Halloween at work! Cute! Fun! Nice! Then one of Lacey's coworkers, Bea, says, "I think I'm gonna dress up as an African

---

1   I can't believe it took me this long to mention Anita Baker.

voodoo priest!" Boo. Not fun. Bad. She goes on to explain how she is going to paint her face black and put a bone through her nose. And, just like that, a rare happy work conversation turns back into the usual nightmare. Lacey says, "You cannot do that." The woman goes on to explain that she once went to a wedding whose *theme* was African Voodoo Priest. "They all dressed up like that!" Now, I know that racism runs rampant in America. I know that white people love crazy Black stereotypes. I know they can't see how it may be wrong to put a bone through your nose, but, y'all. A wedding? Lacey cannot believe it. She goes to their boss and explains what happened. The boss is livid. He says, "Blatant ignorance like that on display at my workplace? Absolutely not." He storms into the room where everyone is gathered and says, "All you racist SOBs are fired!" Did I get ya? Did you believe me for a second? Ha ha! Sorry. It's just fun to do. That didn't happen. Lacey did tell her boss, not because the boss would do anything, but because it was the right thing to do. So the boss does nothing and the woman comes to work with her face painted black and a bone through her nose. Lacey took a picture of her and texted it to me and we aren't allowed to put it in this book. And, honestly, that's for the best. Pretty bad story, but here's the kicker: Bea's husband is a Black man.

4-H: WHY DID I EVER THINK COMING HERE WITH MY CHILD WAS A GOOD IDEA?

This is the story of the first and last time Lacey took her child to a place where she knew she might encounter racists. Okay, so for those of you who don't know, there's this thing called 4-H. It puts on an event like a county fair—sort of. You know that thing where kids compete to see who has the best goat or see who can hog-tie a pig? Country stuff like that. It's a big event with a lot of people and everyone has fun.

Lacey used to work at a girls' home and she would take a big group of multicultural teenagers to the fair, and they'd all pet cows, have a caramel apple and a generally giggly time. The teachers would wear green polos and the children would wear white polos. Even though most of the participants are farmers and their children, they were seemingly okay with having an array of minorities from the girls' home there. They went every year, and Lacey knew exactly who to talk to. Some of the farmers delighted in seeing the girls and talking to them about their livestock. A lot of the people were so nice that Lacey thought, *That's what I get for thinking these girls would be unsafe at an event like this. Shame on me*. We think the reason everyone was so nice is that, even though the farmers and country kids were not what I like to call "interracially socialized," they liked being like, "Look, girls from the girls' home, this is a sheep! We shave its wool like this and blah blah I'm teaching you poor souls" kind of deal. Also, Lacey was okay bringing the girls from the home there because she knew she wouldn't have to worry about them having to take shit from anyone. Side story:

At the girls' home, Lacey would sit in the back of the classes sometimes to keep an eye on things. The teachers would sometimes have them watch videos in their classes. They were always unbearably boring except for this one perfect day. The teacher, an old white lady, insisted they learn about musicals! Lacey was so happy to watch something at work that she would've been watching anyway. Lacey and I love musicals. Fun fact: The top three movie musicals are:

Dreamgirls
Flower Drum Song
Seven Brides for Seven Brothers

Don't press me on that. I said it's a fact. Anyway, this PBS special about the history of musicals is narrated by Julie Andrews! Yay! It starts in ancient Greece and goes through England and gets to vaudeville, at which point Lacey thinks, *Uh-oh*. She realizes they may see some blackface. Now, these girls have been shit on their whole lives and they fend for themselves. If this old white lady shows them a special that glorifies blackface, a fucking well-deserved riot is gonna break out. Lacey is sweating bullets. Then, much to her dismay, there's a whole section about Al Jolson, the famous blackface guy! (I wanted to spell-check his name but I won't for fear I'll have to look at some crap.)

Vaudeville blackface acts, like most blackface acts, were where people painted their faces black and pretended to be buffoons. One famous blackface act is a farmer looking for two Black people as they hide in the chicken coop. The farmer yells, "Are you guys in there?" And the Black guys yell, "Ain't nobody here but us chickens!" 'Cause they were sooooo stuuuupid. Blackface helped white people devalue Black people and see us as a bunch of idiots. I don't want to get into why blackface is bad. No one who thinks it's good got this far in this book. But if you liked this paragraph, please keep an eye out for my next public-speaking engagement called "Blackface and the

Origins of Black Comedy." It explores the effect the white gaze has had on the representation of Black people in mainstream comedy. It's available by getting in a time machine and listening to what I scream into my pillow between 2005 and 2010. Back to the story.

The girls are watching these idiots dancing around in black-face and start looking around like, "What the hell is this?" Lacey thinks, *Okay. I'm sure this show is going to comment about how this is now considered offensive and people have evolved or something at the end of the fucking blackface section of this shit show*. But the show seems to be praising Al Jolson. Gulp. Suddenly, the narrator, Julie Andrews, appears. Lacey is relieved. Surely Julie Andrews will save us. This woman said something to the effect of, "Some people are offended by blackface but there is nothing offensive about it." Now, the kids are out-and-out talking to each other like, "What did this hoe say?" The teacher pauses the video to calm them down. Lacey is relieved. The old white teacher says, "There's nothing wrong with blackface." Le sigh. Lacey takes the teacher out into the hallway and explains to her that she's an idiot. The lady doesn't relent. Lacey takes the video out, throws it away, and replaces it with a video about pollination. Lacey came home and told me this story and, small world, that's the same lady who used to be a drama teacher a million years ago who told my friend's mom she couldn't play Maria in *West Side Story* because her "skin was too dark." Too dark. To play. Maria. OKAAAAYYYY.

Back to wherever we were. Lacey is at 4-H with people from work. They all came in a group with their kids! It's a fun outing. This is the first time she's been there without her green polo and group of mostly minority children. Lacey is with her child, Imani, and she's extremely young. Four or five. Imani is enjoying all the animals and the fun food. Lacey sees one of those boards where you put your head through and take a picture and you're like a mermaid and a fisherman or a cow and a farmer—stuff like that. But this one is where you can be a Black prisoner and a white guard. It's next to a stand where you can meet your local policemen. Their stand says, "Talk to us!" I think the fuck not.

As they enjoy themselves, they happen upon something called the Animal Scramble. It's where a bunch of little kids are put in a fenced-off area with a bunch of baby animals and if they catch one, they get to keep it! Even city kids can participate! If you can't keep your animal, you can give it to someone who can! Lacey texts her friends so they can come watch her daughter be cute. Lacey goes up to the guy to register. And what luck! It's one of the nice farmers who loves to give the girls from the home a long-winded explanation about the gestation of baby calves. He's one of the sweetest guys in the whole place.

Lacey: Hello! How have you been?

Farmer: What do you want?

This is a real surprise. This farmer is the nice one! He was so sweet and helpful. But now he's regular old racist-style grossed out by Lacey. This man does not recognize her. She's not with a bunch of minority children and she is without her green polo. To him, she's a random Black lady.

Lacey: I'd like to enter my daughter in the Animal Scramble!

Farmer: You can't do it.

Lacey: What? Why?

Farmer: It's for people who live in our community. It's not for people like you. It isn't *for you*.

Lacey analyzes the situation. If pressed, this man will get crazy and she's with her kid and there are cops around the corner. Lacey's hands are tied. She has no choice but to silently leave. She doesn't want to get so mad she murders this guy and brings that prisoner/guard photo op to life. And she doesn't want this guy to have the satisfaction of seeing that not getting to participate hurts her and her daughter's feelings. She's got no choice but to scoop up the child and get out. As they head to the car, Lacey looks back and sees her friends waiting in the audience to watch her child participate in the Animal Scramble. She texts them, "Sorry, we had to leave. We went to the movies." Then they went to the movies.

Bit of a depressing story, innit? (I've been watching BBC.) Sorry. You'll find that a lot of these stories don't have a natural conclusion or a "what I learned" at the end of them. That is because this is real life and it does not stop. These stories only reaffirm where we are. They don't shine a light on anything new. Here's a better one about that home:

When Lacey worked at the girls' home, people thought it was mostly Black girls there, but that wasn't the case. There were a lot of white girls. And when you got there, all the hair products they gave you would be white hair products. You would get hair spray, gel, and white-people shampoo and conditioner. So the Black staff looked around and noticed the Black girls couldn't maintain their hair with what they were given. They didn't even have the right tools. Brushes, combs, etc. A group of them went to the higher-ups and told them about it. They were told that Black hair products were a privilege. That's right. The white kids could get whatever they needed for their upkeep, but the Black kids had to suffer. Looks like Black hair products aren't the privilege, but being white is. The Black employees and the higher-ups went back and forth for a while. But eventually the girls won their right to have hair products. This story took place in 1969. Just kidding, but doesn't that make it make more sense? Okay, back to sillier stories.

Lacey and her friend, who is a giant bodybuilder, are at Walmart. Lacey is a bodybuilder, too, but she's also a little lady, so you can't really tell when you look at her. But this guy looks like a frigging Black Arnold Schwarzenegger. He's huge. The two of them are having trouble with the self-checkout. There's an old white lady behind them who is very upset. She's huffing and puffing, which is insane because Lacey's friend is comically intimidating. She then rams her shopping cart into his foot. They both see it. They both are taken aback by it. They both assess the situation.

Him: I'm not gonna say anything.

Lacey: I will. I'll only get six months, but if you say anything, you'll get shot.

They laugh and laugh and the situation becomes funny. This woman is mumbling and grumbling and they choose to ignore her. She clearly wants a fight. The longer they stand there, the louder she gets. It's hilarious. They're fumbling with the self-checkout and it's making the lady behind them so mad! They start giggling at the ridiculousness of it, which makes her madder. Shit is getting tense! People are starting to notice that this white lady wants these two Black people to acknowledge her. Even though it's a little difficult, Lacey and her friend are chill. Giggly, but chill. Right before they would have had to say something, the register works and they are free! They bolt out of there. That was a close one. Lacey has never seen this behavior before. Like, you've seen it in movies where the white people try to pick a fight with the Black people because they know the Black people can't do anything because they'd go to jail forever. But to pull this type of stuff today? Brave. And in a Walmart, no less. It seems like people get their asses beat in Walmarts every dang day! Google "Walmart beatdown" and see how many pages there are of videos. Wait. Don't do that. Your computer will think you like watching people get beat up. And every day it'll be another tank top brawl where a boob pops out.

On the way out, they stop to get water out of the vending machine that's in the part of the store where the carts are. As they're standing there, they see Lacey's white friend Emily. Lacey tells Emily about writing this book. Emily is shocked. They tell her what just happened in line. The three of them laugh about it. Emily can't believe that happened. But, you know, she *can*. She leaves.

As they stand there, getting water, the crazy lady rolls by cursing them out at full volume. Lacey and her giant friend laugh and laugh. Then—and this is fairly common—the second this old crazy lady is out of range, she yells the n-word a million times. "They're n*****s! Fucking filthy n*****s!" She had herself a full-blown racial-epithet meltdown. And this is in a Black neighborhood. The bravery this woman has. Lacey texts Emily later that day. "You will never believe what happened. The crazy lady came out and started screaming at us yelling racial slurs!" Emily replies, "I saw her! I wondered if it was the same lady!"

About a week later, it was time for a funtime lunch with Lacey and her coworkers! It's better than sitting at your desk working, but not as good because you are left vulnerable to all manner of insane comments. And, being the only Black person there, you can be sure they're coming. So, as the lunch goes on, the conversation is fun. Lacey's having a really good time. Everyone starts to talk about where they're from. A coworker begins talking and Lacey can see where this is going.

"I'm from a small town and Omaha is scary."

When white people say "Omaha is scary," they mean "There's a lot of Black people." I know how ridiculous this must sound to anyone from a bigger city, but that is what small-town Nebraskans think of Omaha. And she doesn't stop there. "There's a lotta diversity. Diversity is scary." Yes, she did—she just called diversity scary! What she means is "I don't like being around minorities." Lacey is calm. She knew this fun lunch wasn't gonna last long.

You see, it's when you're having the most fun that people say the most fucked-up things. They're feeling loose, ready to let their hair down, they see you're in a good mood. It's time to say something racist and see if you can get away with it.

Lacey says, "Did you just say diversity is scary? What are you talking about? How is diversity scary? Why would you say that?" This lady goes, "When my kids started school here, they were scared because Black people are mean."

To remind you: Lacey is Black. She is the only Black person at this table and, clearly, she is the only Black person in this woman's life. Lacey goes, "You can't say that. You can't make blanket statements about Black people. It shows how ignorant you are. You don't know any Black people. You have no idea how they are. It would be like if I said all British people walk with a limp. I don't know any British people. Seen some on TV, met a few, but I don't *know* any. So, if I said that in front of a British person, imagine how ignorant I would sound."

Now, at this exact moment, Emily, Lacey's white friend from

Walmart, walks by. She sees Lacey and comes up to the table and happily chirps, "Lacey! Oh my gosh, you're every-where I go! How's the book coming along!" Lacey says, "It's going great! Every day I have something new to add to it!" Emily walks away and Lacey's coworkers ask what her book is about. Lacey says, "It's about growing up Black in Omaha and the crazy things that white people say to me." There is a long pause where everyone realizes the danger they're in.

And I'd just like to take this time to tell any Black people who are reading this, you should tell everyone you know that you're writing a book just like this one. It has truly come in handy more than it should have.

AND NOW, IT'S TIME TO PLAY "GUESS THE THEME OF THESE STORIES"!

Story 1!
Once, Lacey was going to a special ceremony at church. They had all dressed up and were ready for fun. She and her boyfriend are in the Taco Bell parking lot, eating the food they'd just ordered. A cop walks up to them and taps on the window. Her boyfriend rolls the window down. The cop's attitude is like he caught them red-handed, but they're just sitting there eating. The cop goes, "What's going on here?" They explain they're eating Taco Bell, like kids do. "What's in your cup there, son?" He explains it's Pepsi, the Choice of a New Generation. The cop turns to Lacey. "What did you just hide under your seat?" What? "I just saw you put something under

your seat." Lacey says, "I didn't but you can look under there if you like." The cop grows bored of talking to them and says, "Ugh. You need to take her back where you got her from." He thought she was a prostitute! This is what she was wearing:

"I'M THE FANCIEST PROSTITUTE ALIIIIIIIIIVE!"

Story 2!

So, when I was very young and cute, I was all ready to go out dancing with my girlfriends. I had on black velvet bell-bottoms, a blue velvet long-sleeved top, and blue platform heels. I know it sounds like a lot, but that's because it is a lot and I am a lot. It was my favorite outfit for a long time. I'm picking up my white male friend, who is wearing a suit. On the way home we pass by a truck stop and he wants to see if his dad is in town. So—and this is what makes us suspicious—we drive slowly up and down along the semis, looking at their license plates to see if we can find his. Again, a white man in a suit and a Black woman in head-to-toe velvet and platforms drive slowly up and down the aisles of a truck stop. Soon, a police officer taps on our window. My friend rolls it down and you would have thought my friend was the king of England. The respect this cop had for this white man in a suit is un-frigging-matched. I did not know cops acted like that. My friend explains what we are doing there. The cop explains that he stopped us because there's been a lot of prostitution. This cop thinks I am a prostitute! I try to explain that we aren't trick and hoe. But the cop is wholly uninterested in listening to me and seems to be grossed out that he has to talk to me in the first place and tells us to leave. It all starts to take a while and my friend becomes annoyed by the cop—and the cop can tell! "You don't have anything on us. You have to let us go." And I am like, *This is how I die. I die because my white friend talked to the cops like he lost his fool mind.* But instead the cop is like, "Okay, but you guys have to leave." We are saved. As we start to drive away, my friend reminds the cop that I am not a prostitute. I don't know why he did that, because the cop did not believe him. If this had been a different cop or maybe even this cop on a different day, I might still be in jail for being a prostitute. Think about it: We would have said *nu-uh*. The cop would have said *yes-huh*, and we would have gone to jail.

Story 3!
Lacey, Pastor Frank, and two Black women friends went to the airport to pick someone up. The mood was light and they were having a blast. As they're skipping and giggling along the airport arrivals area, the girls all linked arms with each other and then folded Pastor Frank into the Laverne and Shirley fun. When they linked arms with him, he recoiled and snarked, "Don't do that, they're gonna think you're prostitutes!"

Okay, have you guessed the theme of these stories? You're right! The theme is Mistaken Identity!

RACIST MAGICIAN

Lacey hired a magician for her office Christmas Party. She saw him on the Internet and thought, *He's funny!* She was wrong. In order to fully immerse yourself in this story, you need to know that most of the staff were people of color.

The magician gets there and is greeted by Lacey. They exchange pleasantries and he gets to work. All he has to do is exactly what Lacey saw him do in the video and people will love it. He looks out at his predominately Black audience and starts off his show by saying, "I hope you guys find me funny. I'm all the way from Ralston and you guys have a different kind of humor over here." Now, what he meant by that was, Black people live far away from Ralston and they don't like the same jokes as white people. And he believed what he said because, instead of doing his act the way he normally does, he improvises a zillion Black jokes. Old, stereotype-driven, horrible jokes about Black people to Black people from a man looking at his first-ever group of Black people. His act included the following jokes:

"What are you guys eating? Popeyes chicken?"

He asked a lady a math question that no one would get. It was part of the trick. When she couldn't answer he snarked, "That's Omaha Public Schools for ya!"

There's a buffet. People are getting food and sitting down the whole show. While he's doing a trick, a Black lady gets up to get food. He remarks, "Whoa, you look like you just wandered in off the street. Hey! Quit stealing food!"

"Even though I'm from Ralston, I know how to dab!
dabs incorrectly

It was a horrible show and no one had fun. Some would blame the magician for being racist. I blame Lacey for hiring a magician.

I fully accept your blame and vow to do better in the future.

BLACK HISTORY SHOWDOWN

As this book comes to an end, I want you to know I've saved the best story for last. Okay, it might not be the best, but when I think of racism, I think of this story. It's the first story of racism that I can remember hearing and I feel like as you grow up and the world tries to convince you that racism is you overreacting, I would remember this story and know that I had to be on my own side. Take us home, Lacey!

When I was a senior in high school, my African American history class entered a team of students into the Black History Showdown. It was a contest among Midwest students to test their knowledge of Black history. The contest was held in Dubuque, Iowa, of all places. Around that same time there were cross burnings happening there. A teacher told us they were trying to change the face of their town and show they were accepting of other races. There was one other Black team at this competition. The rest of the teams were all white. It was filmed in a game-show-style setting. Filmed for what or by whom, I have no idea. But there were plenty of cameras there and a nice setup.

If, by any chance, you read this story and think you may know where this footage is, please let me know. I would kill to see it.

The competition was basically this: Everyone was asked questions and the first to use their buzzer could answer. The audience was all white, filled mostly by the parents of the other players. The Black children's parents weren't in attendance both because it was far from where they lived and because they probably had to work. I know mine did. The competition started with some easy questions and, gradually, the questions became harder. But even when they were easy, the Black children dominated. The audience started to become upset as our team began answering most of the questions. Parents began angrily storming out as it became clear that we would be the winners. It was strange to look out at a sea of white angry faces. And, not to be rude, but who cares who wins this competition? Especially if you guys are racist? What does it matter that you don't know who Frederick Douglass is if you don't like civil rights? Who knows. Toward the end of the competition, things are getting tense. We are winning, and each of these last questions is making the audience groan with disappointment. When, like a ray of hope, an easy question is asked—"Who wrote the famous 'I Have a Dream' speech?"—everyone is on the edge of their seats. Surely the other teams would have the answer for this one. All they had to do is ring the buzzer first, answer correctly, and not be an embarrassment. A white student buzzed in and, beaming, answered, "Malcom X!" Can you imagine what Malcolm X's "I Have a Dream" speech would be? I think it's safe to say that's a totally different dream. The thought is hilarious. So this kid really blows it and there was a snicker heard from some of the white students who had already been eliminated. That infuriated the crowd. All of a sudden, one of the judges, an old white man, stormed the stage and took the mic from the host. He yelled "Stop filming!" He assumed that we, being the Black kids, were the ones who laughed, but we did not. He proceeded to have a full-throated public racist meltdown for the ages. This man went on to tell the Black students that "everyone knows white kids are smarter than Black kids; everyone knows this." He emphasized that several times, saying, "You should be happy you were even invited to this event." He was really trying to make the angry parents and audience members calm down and stay. Before turning the cameras back on, he took most of our points away. He explained to us that we would not be the winners that day. We weren't going to win because it's "just not right." One of the white teams ended up winning. We went home and that's it. That's the story.

You made it! You made it to the end of a crazy book about the experiences of one tiny lady. Again, I'd like to say this is not every experience and it is not a lifetime's worth of stories. And, with that said, isn't it waaaay more than you expected? Even me, knowing most of these stories before we started this book, looking back on them I'm like, "Daaaang, that's a lot of stories!" 'Cause I can see not only the stories we didn't have room for but also the stories that we had to leave out! It's a lot.

We are not into trying to educate white America, but maybe we accidentally did. Maybe white readers learned that just because your Black friends aren't sitting you down, going over all their trauma with you, doesn't mean it doesn't exist! Maybe you learned that racist stuff happens all the time. Maybe you've become emboldened to speak up when you see someone being a racist piece of shit. Maybe you've realized the racist piece of shit was you! I don't know. I don't know you like that.

And if you're Black and got all the way to the end of this book, thank you. Thanks for walking through these personal and silly and dumb experiences with us. I know it may have brought up some hard shit, but it made us feel heard and worth your time. We want you to know that we support you in whatever decisions you make in situations like these. It is a lot to ask people to live in a place that would treat them like this AND ask them to be in charge of fixing it. People are just trying to cope. Having said that, if you feel like hurting some feelings, do it! If you feel like fighting for what you believe in, do it! If you feel like calling in sick, do it! Write down your grievances and put them in a book! Whatever! Do you! Truly, we are all just trying to get by.

What our secret hope is is that this book has given you the courage to never stop telling these stories. At almost every job I've ever had, it always got to the point that whenever people saw me coming they would say, "Here comes Lacey about to say something racist happened." And they were right. I did. And sometimes I got fired and sometimes I didn't. But I always did exactly what I wanted to do when I wanted to do it. I would also like to say it's sad that people feel, in this day and age, that they have to remain silent. And every situation is different, but I'd like to invite you to the possibility that remaining silent is no longer a requirement.

Thanks for going on this journey with us. In closing, I'd just like to say: Can you believe this shit?

Keep an eye out for our next book: *Lacey's Horrible Outfit Choices!* It'll be a picture book.

Oh my god shut up. We mean, thank you for reading the book. It means a lot. Please take all these stories and use them.

THE END (of racism). (Just kidding.)

One last thing. I do not possess the ability to be embarrassed by photos, but Lacey does. So enjoy this gem from when we used to sing gospel music together!